HOW TO TEACH COLLEGE

Also by James W. Loewen

Sundown Towns

Lies My Teacher Told Me

Lies Across America

Lies My Teacher Told Me About Christopher Columbus

Lies My Teacher Told Me: Young Readers' Edition

Teaching What Really Happened

The Mississippi Chinese: Between Black and White

HOW TO
TEACH COLLEGE

INSPIRING DIVERSE STUDENTS
IN CHALLENGING TIMES

JAMES W. LOEWEN

EDITED BY NICHOLAS LOEWEN AND
MICHAEL DAWSON

NEW YORK
LONDON

Requests for permission to reproduce selections from this book should be made through our
website: https://thenewpress.com/contact.

Published in the United States by The New Press, New York, 2025
Distributed by Two Rivers Distribution

ISBN 978-1-62097-920-4 (hc)
ISBN 978-1-62097-939-6 (ebook)
CIP data is available

The New Press publishes books that promote and enrich public discussion and understanding
of the issues vital to our democracy and to a more equitable world. These books are made
possible by the enthusiasm of our readers; the support of a committed group of donors, large
and small; the collaboration of our many partners in the independent media and the not-for-
profit sector; booksellers, who often hand-sell New Press books; librarians; and above all by
our authors.

www.thenewpress.com

Book design by Bookbright Media
Composition by Bookbright Media
This book was set in Adobe Garamond and Mundial Narrow

Printed in the United States of America

10 9 8 7 6 5 4 3 2 1

Contents

HOW TO TEACH COLLEGE

Foreword

My Dad as a Teacher

NICHOLAS LOEWEN

Growing up, my sister and I learned not to say anything when something around the house wasn't working. We would halt ourselves mid-sentence: "Dad? This door doesn't cl—" "Hey, Dad, the fire in the wood-burning stove isn't—" We knew that if we finished the sentence, he would take our question as an opportunity to teach us how to adjust the hinges on a door so that it closed completely, or how to adjust the flue in the wood-burning stove so the fire would draw efficiently. Of course, as a kid, I didn't always want the lesson or the knowledge. I just wanted him to fix it.

But my father was a consummate teacher in both his professional and personal life. Some of my earliest memories are of him teaching me things. Teaching me to dive into a pool, teaching me to use woodworking tools, teaching me to catch crickets for fishing trips. I recently learned a new word—*heuristic*—which describes teaching in a way that enables someone to discover something on their own, and I think Dad was an expert at helping me discover things myself. Of course, it annoyed the hell out of me—I just wanted to have the thing done. But my father was a big proponent of personal competence.

Even more essentially, my father was a learner. He stands out in my life as the person who knew the most, about the most—he was expert in his knowledge of classical music, owning thousands of albums of classical performances. He knew the constellations and would stop on nighttime drives to point them out to us with a flashlight. He knew which wild mushrooms to pick and eat from the woods, and even sold them to local restaurants. From his years as a Boy Scout, he knew how to camp and canoe. He designed and built an entire house essentially by himself in the early 1970s in Jackson, Mississippi, that still stands today.

Although he was a sociologist by training, Dad also knew literature well, once identifying the Swiss author of the play I was teaching: "That's Dürrenmatt, right?" he asked. He was a chemistry major before switching to sociology, and therefore well-versed in the physical sciences, too. He made the same joking interjection throughout my entire life—"Moholy-Nagy!" instead of "Holy cow!" How many folks even know of the Hungarian polymath László Moholy-Nagy? When Dad was a professor at the University of Vermont, he audited a class on car maintenance at the agricultural school. This thirst for catholic knowledge was impressive, inspirational, aspirational, and frustrating. He won arguments with me on sports and politics, on physics and literature. He was the person I would go to with questions on nearly anything, because he had extensive knowledge about nearly everything (it seemed) and retained it forever. All of this is to say that he learned it and remembered it, used it, shared it, and then learned more. He was a researcher, an archivist, an activist, and an intellectual.

At my father's first teaching job, at Tougaloo College, a historically Black institution in Mississippi, he met his mentor Ernst Borinski, a sociologist who had fled the Holocaust and become a professor at the school in the 1950s. Borinski had a maxim my dad took to heart: "What a man doesn't know, you must teach him." Dad recounts in these pages and also in another of his books the instructive moment at Tougaloo that changed his career. During one of his classes, he learned that his students had deeply absorbed the lies they had been taught about the Reconstruction era following the Civil War. Given his training as a sociologist, he easily imagined the corrosive impact that learning such falsehoods had on Black and white students alike. This experience motivated him to set out to expose people to what they didn't know about American history, to help them become better and more competent citizens. Thus was born his best-selling book *Lies My Teacher Told Me*, a book Dad hoped would help high school teachers become better instructors.

Growing up with such a parent helped to instill in me the importance of reflection and study, and especially the excitement of learning. As often happens in families, I followed in my father's footsteps and became a teacher. When I began teaching high school, my father's most important piece of advice to me was to have high expectations for my students. This was an important element of his parenting, too. Of course, this attitude is not a panacea for a son's lassitude. In eighth grade, I was able to confound his expectations and nearly fail the year. But I knew that learning and being learn*ed* were sacrosanct values in our family, and I absorbed and held on to those values, even when I wasn't living up to them.

Now, as a parent and a teacher, I see that there is not really a huge difference between teaching and parenting. In both cases, one instructs children to help them better understand their world, to help them become better people, and to share with them the things that are most important. That was another key thing my father taught me:

Our role in our short lives is to be good people, to help others, and to live a good story. And to raise good dogs (he loved Labrador retrievers).

Many of the things I learned from my dad I use with my own children and in my high school teaching. Of course, many techniques I use in the classroom also help with my parenting. I saw that in providing lessons to my children, I needed to do what my father called "scaffolding": They didn't know how to sweep a floor well just because I explained it to them once; I needed to model it, give them small tasks to build into complex ones, create steps and chunks of instruction, and give them positive feedback that they could then put to use soon after receiving it. And, as my dad discusses in this book, such scaffolding also applies to the classroom. If I just tell my ninth graders to write a paper, some will have the a priori knowledge and experience to construct a passable piece of writing. But most will not do good work without modeling, chunking, positive feedback, and practice.

In the last years of his life, my father mentioned to me he was working on this manuscript on teaching and asked me if I was interested in undertaking its completion. After he died in 2021, I finally took the time to read through it. While some chapters were whole, others contained unfinished explanations. They contained references to anecdotes, some of which I recognized from stories he told me; exercises, lessons, and assessments in classes he'd used; and brief swatches of ideas, colleagues, and assignments that I could at times piece together either from instances he had recounted to me (or sometimes assigned to me!). With the considerable help of Michael Dawson, an author and a lecturer in sociology at Portland Community College with whom my dad corresponded about this project, I've been able to hone his incomplete manuscript into a book that distills some of his best, most original thinking on how to teach well.

I've already found the ideas useful in my own teaching. I referred to the manuscript as I prepared my syllabi for my upcoming year teaching high school English. Why am I teaching this novel? I asked myself. What do I love about my subject? Why *wouldn't* I let my students know what I am looking for in an essay?

I hope that college (and high school) teachers will also find this book full of compelling strategies for improving their pedagogy, and that some of the curriculum ideas, assignments, anecdotes, and practical suggestions in this book find a place in your practice in ways that make you a more competent teacher. I'm happy that you're eager to learn more about teaching and to spread your love of your subject to others.

Here, you'll see my dad's respect and high expectations for students as well as for the professors he addresses. You'll feel his deep love of learning and teaching. Overall, what I see throughout the book, and what I hope all who read this book will discover, is his conviction that learning is virtuous, that people want to be virtuous, and that a commitment to lifelong learning allows people—both professors and students—to be both competent and good.

Introduction

Teaching Well

In their 2011 book *Academically Adrift*, sociologists Richard Arum and Josipa Roksa contend that most faculty and most students have forged a Faustian bargain: Professors don't spend much time teaching or preparing to teach, while students don't spend much time in class or studying. *Each goes easy on the other.*[1]

At many colleges, students earn self-esteem and the esteem of others by finding and taking the easiest course on campus. They have "beat the system." They're getting an A with almost no work. Many students who avoid that game still go through college trying mainly to fly below the radar—avoid getting in trouble or even noticed; go through the motions; get B's. That is not a good way to do college. It removes the "why" of higher education. Meanwhile, whatever the course, most students still dread tests and consider them, at best, a necessary evil, a mere way of certifying to the professor that they have learned and, hence, should get a good grade. Finally, after serving their four (or more) years, all across the nation, many students graduate but can't write well, speak well, reason clearly, or marshal information (whether qualitative or quantitative) effectively. Surely those are key goals and, therefore, key failings.

Also surely, these failings often reach even deeper: Learning *how* to learn is more important than possessing knowledge—even skills—that may become obsolete. Even into the first two decades of this century, many of us knew people in computer programming, computer graphics, website creation, online security, and other related fields who never used a computer in college because they didn't yet exist. Their undergraduate degrees were as likely to be in Spanish or religion as in math or business. Many students will have several careers over their lifetime, and the subject of their major may not help them prepare in any specific way for their first one. This process will only accelerate, and this rapid pace of change will only engender a quandary. Many students want to major in something that promises a job. They do not realize that the economy is changing so rapidly that it's hard to predict what jobs will be like in ten years, let alone twenty.

What is constant is that college graduates need, above all else, to be lifelong learners. They need to buy books, even books not required for a class. Or, in our perhaps bookless future, they need to learn new things and to want to learn new things, even things not required for a class. They need to be critical thinkers. They need to be able to read and critique a table or chart. Many will need to be able, in fact, to create that table and complete it with the correct percentages. Most will need to understand basic statistics. Many will need to do evaluation research. *All* will need to be able to write powerfully, give convincing presentations, conduct effective interviews, and work well in groups.

A crucial component of critical thinking goes by several names. Psychologists call it "metacognition." Historians call it "historiography." Sociologists call it the "sociology of knowledge."[2] In philosophy, it's "epistemology." We might call it "thinking about how we think." Assumptions are built into the way we think about things within a given subject—even into the way we *see* things. If we don't examine those assumptions, we cannot see their limitations. Metacognition is central not just to a liberal arts education but to anything that might deserve to be called a "higher" education.

In some ways, our new connectivity has made matters even worse. Now students in some college classes spend much of their time texting or on social media on their laptops or phones, being present in the room in body only. Even at elite colleges, professors can no longer count on docile students willing to take notes assiduously and dependably learning what the professor presents, no matter how monotonous the presentation.

We college teachers have our own parallel list of sins, and we are the ones who set the rules and standards. At many colleges and universities, the relationship between students and faculty remains faintly adversarial, as if students are somehow trying to "get away" with something, unless "we" prevent that. That makes for a poor job of educating. The *Academically Adrift* authors note that more than 45 percent of students they observed showed no "significant improvement" in measures of critical reading and thinking during the first two years of college.[3]

More than a few professors teach solely because they have to, so they can do what they *really* want to do, which is "their work"—their research, their writing.[4] Too many professors at too many research institutions and wannabe research institutions do all they can to limit their teaching. They bargain their courseload down to four courses per year or less—sometimes much less. They recycle old course outlines, which might be okay if the courses were good, but they do so without even adding new examples to make their courses resonate with today's issues. They use media, technology, and old lecture notes to cut their preparation time to a few minutes per class. By the third week, they forget what they posted as their office hours the first week, because they never ask students to come, and no students do.

Those professors miss the joys of teaching. Because they teach so seldom, they may never see a student in a second course. When they do, they may not recognize her, having not learned her name or anything meaningful about her the first time, which also means they cannot notice how her mind has developed and how, perhaps, they played an important role in the process. No one says to them, "This course was so great! What are you teaching next term?" No one asks them if they'll be around on Commencement Day so they can bring their parents by to say hello. They also miss out on the warm recollections that mentoring can bring at class reunions from alumni who make an effort to seek out their favorite professors years later.

Introductory courses suffer the most from faculty avoidance. Many departments belittle first-year courses and staff them with adjuncts. "At many colleges and universities," writes Roger Martin, former president of Randolph-Macon College,

> first-year students take large introductory courses in classes of 100 or more. Teaching is usually done by an instructor lecturing in front of the classroom while students dutifully take notes later to be regurgitated on a quiz. There is very little class participation involving discussion and debate. Writing anything over a few pages is unusual.[5]

Such pedagogy is shortsighted. Many colleges face terrible attrition between students' first and second years. First-year courses like the ones Martin describes are undoubtedly a reason for that.

*   *   *

And let's be honest: Most college professors make a *much* bigger impact on the world through their teaching than through their research. Not true for Einstein, but true for most.

It's an old and deep problem.

When I was a college student, most college professors knew nothing about teaching. They just taught. By that I mean they talked to us for fifty minutes (if the class met on Monday, Wednesday, and Friday) or seventy-five minutes (if it met on Tuesday and Thursday). If they finished before the class ended, which was rare, they asked, "Any questions?" That was it! They weren't supposed to know anything about how to teach. They were supposed to know their subject matter and convey it to us.

To be sure, they also gave us tests. Most courses had midterm and final exams; some also had quizzes. Typically, the midterm took up one class session and consisted of multiple-choice questions followed by an essay question. The final was longer and consisted of more multiple-choice questions and two or three essay questions. Typically, we didn't get the finals back. We could leave a self-addressed stamped envelope, but we didn't know how much postage was required. Besides, we were usually happy just to be done with the semester.

Professors knew nothing about testing, either. Again, they weren't supposed to. They were supposed to know their subject matter, and that was supposed to suffice as preparation for asking and grading questions about it.

Back then, even the idea that college students *should* be taught effectively was a foreign thought. Maybe teachers in community colleges needed to know how to teach, but *real* college students were supposed to learn no matter what kind of teacher they had. The situation might be summed up by a put-down a vice president of the Woodrow Wilson Foundation made in the mid-1960s while speaking about college teaching to a bunch of newly minted college graduates, including me. He had just given a dry talk that itself consisted of a lecture, followed by, "Any questions?" His talk had not contained any actual tips about *how* to teach in college, so an audience member asked him if he had any. He dismissed the question scornfully: "You mean, like, 'Leave a clean board?' *There!*" And that was the sum of his suggestions.

As graduate students morphed into new professors, they had few resources for doing better. Graduate students in physics took courses in physics. Graduate students in sociology, like me, took courses in sociology. Indeed, when I took a course in political science from a rather famous Harvard professor, doing so was unusual, yet no discipline is closer to sociology than political science. Certainly, no graduate students in physics, sociology, or any other discipline in the College of Arts and Sciences ventured over to the Harvard School of Education to take a course there. For that matter, the "Ed School" did not even *offer* a course on how to teach college.

Today, most graduate students who plan to be college professors still never take a course on how to teach physics, sociology, or any other discipline. Harvard's Ed School still does not offer a regular core course on how to teach college, though it does now have an occasional specialty seminar.[6] In *Academically Adrift*, published in 2011, the authors wrote: "During graduate training, future faculty members receive little if any formal instruction on teaching." A 2015 article in the *Chronicle of Higher Education* could still state, as a matter of course, that graduate programs "are notorious for not teaching Ph.D.s about pedagogy." At most universities, graduate students learn not to value teaching. They see peers getting dismissed for failing "prelims" or for writing inadequate dissertations, but no one flunks out—indeed, no one *can* flunk out—for teaching poorly.[7]

After they get the doctorate, most professors still don't talk about teaching, write about teaching, or read about teaching. When they do think about teaching, often they do so defensively, in their minds dismissing popular teachers as "panderers to students" or "easy graders."

We are, in short, failing our students as teachers.

This cannot and should not stand. The old style of college teaching won't do. It never *did* do. Every theory of learning and countless empirical studies of what works in education show that most students do not learn efficiently simply from being talked to in traditional classrooms. Maybe no one does. Certainly, students find incessant lecturing boring. If students are docile enough, professors may not notice they are boring, at least not until the final exam, and then they may simply blame students for the bad performance, which, thanks to the reigning compact of complacency, plagues and diminishes the college endeavor. Thus does the wheel of mediocrity keep turning.

And make no mistake, we college teachers are the gatekeepers here. Instead of blaming students, and instead of letting them "get away with" so little studying and thinking, professors need to become partners-in-learning with their students. We must exude the expectation that students in turn will be partners-in-learning with us. Above all, we must assail and transcend the reigning compact of complacency, which does to higher education what milquetoast textbooks and stultifying expectations have long done to high school history students. (See here my book *Lies My Teacher Told Me!*)

Our duty to try harder and be smarter arises from the seriousness of our enterprise, the importance of our subject matter, the collective formation of a supportive critiquing group, our demand that no student fail because we are in this together, and out of sheer respect for each and every student.

My hopes for this book are modest. I hope you will find in it at least a few nitty-gritty ideas that are convincing enough that you try them yourself and then embrace them. Maybe one of my ideas on how to teach will win you over. Maybe you'll like the "concentric circles" way of sparking discussion, early in the semester. Maybe . . . no, I'll stop here and get on with the task of introducing my ideas for your consideration and perhaps your adoption.

The Teachers That Students Need

Surely your number one reason for being in the classroom is to help students learn. Surely you are not there to show off, to contrast your knowledge with their ignorance. Perhaps you are partly there to separate good students from the bad by letter grade, rewarding the former and inducing the latter to leave your department, if not the entire university. If you think doing so *is* part of your job description or your reason for teaching, imagine for a moment that you made your course quite demanding yet taught it so effectively that every student met its demands and earned at least a strong B. Wouldn't that be more satisfying than differentiating them and giving C's, D's, and F's to the bad ones?

So, you want to help students—each and all of them—to learn. Let's consider what "help students to learn" means. Content is part of it, but only part. When students leave my course in introductory sociology, there are some things I want them to know. For instance, I want them to recall some basic social facts, such as what the Black population of the United States is, and also that the general population is and has long been about 51 percent female. To be sure, these facts are easy to find on the web. A good rule is, "If you can Google it, don't teach it." Nonetheless, knowing these facts is useful, partly because many Americans *mis*-know them so drastically. Many of my students at the University of Vermont, for example, imagined that the United States is 20 to 40 percent Black and 60 to 70 percent female. These misconceptions, in turn, lead them to bizarre conclusions when discussing social policy.

More important than knowing mere facts, I want alumni of my "Intro Soc" course to know some concepts, such as the differences between class, status, and power; the meaning of the phrase "sociology of knowledge"; and the marriage terms "endogamy," "exogamy," and "hypergamy." These are a bit harder to learn from a website, especially since I want students not only to know what they mean, but also be able to use them as tools for thinking about social issues.

Nevertheless, that's still just content. More important to me is that students become able to think like sociologists. I recall having a conversation with a friend from college I'll call "Suzie" just to avoid any possible embarrassment, a year after she had graduated. Like me, she had majored in sociology. We were both going through her library, because she was giving me any of her sociology books I wanted since she wasn't going on to work in the field. "Here's *The Sociology of G-E-O-R-G Sigh-mell*," she said, reaching for his anthology. "It's *Simmell*," I replied, referring to an important social theorist in pre–World War I Germany. At this point, Suzie burst out laughing. She had completely forgotten who he was, even how to pronounce his name—yet Simmel had been the topic of her senior paper!

*   *   *

Nevertheless, when I asked her fifty years later, Suzie did not consider her undergraduate education wasted—not even her sociology major. She believed herself able to think sociologically, to make and understand elementary statistical arguments, and to critique false claims made by others. She had needed these skills in all the jobs she had held.

What are *your* course objectives? Are you trying to impart a bundle of knowledge? Do you want your students to know factoids like who Georg Simmel was? Or do you want them to know how to be able to think? To think sociologically, or to think "in" physics, or about poetry? Of course, we want students to know things *and* to think skillfully, but if we had to choose one, would we not choose the thinking skill? Consider the difference between learning something and understanding it. Certainly, you want your students to understand your subject, not merely learn it.

Our broadest goal as faculty members is to help students realize what it is to be an educated person and help them move toward that state. Another important goal for many classes—not just those in sociology and philosophy—is to help students prepare for their jobs as Americans. What is a student's job as an American? Surely it is to help bring into being the America of the future. Doing so requires citizens who are literate and numerate and who can think critically.

In addition to these abilities, it will be well for students and for society if they hold humane values. In today's corporate culture, where Ayn Rand is a commonly read novelist in executive suites, the foregoing statement has become controversial. Nevertheless, it is true. Companies that do well should also do good; companies that do good should do well. Some research shows that this even happens! Management professor Stuart Hart, for example, argues that what he calls "third-generation corporations . . . understand that you make money by doing good things rather than the other way around." Corporate consultants Bassi and McMurrer claim that corporations that do well by their employees also do well for society and usually wind up doing well for their shareholders.[8]

What are "humane values"? What is "good for society"? I'll not answer those weighty questions here, in a book about how to teach, but surely many courses in the humanities and social sciences wrestle with issues that require deep thinking about values. So do courses about such matters as global warming, nuclear power and nuclear war, medical research, genomes, and cosmology.

To become critical thinkers in your discipline, to develop humane values, and to prepare for their individual vocations and for society's needs, today's students need your best teaching efforts. Just delivering content won't do. For that matter, just delivering content won't even prompt students to remember content—not later, after the course is over.

The Joy of Good College Teaching

Serious teaching is required to overcome student resistance and to help students achieve all the outcomes we want them to achieve. Such teaching is not a gift. It is a skill. Therefore, it is learnable. Yes, a pleasant personality helps, but that can be faked. Yes, a sense of humor helps, but one-liners can be memorized.

When you walk into your classroom, you want to feel that there is nowhere else you want to be at that moment. This should be easy. After all, your discipline still inspires you, does it not?

If you want to generate intellectual excitement in your course, in your class, manifest it! Excitement is contagious! Remember back to the day when you first fell in love with your discipline. You *did*, didn't you? Why? What was exciting about it to you? In my own case, it was how chapter 2 in my Intro Soc textbook treated socialization, the process of learning and internalizing the basic folkways and mores of society that all of us go through to become functioning humans and, in our case, Americans. No longer does this excite me much. Now I study and teach about other aspects of sociology. But it did then. When teaching an introductory course, we need to put ourselves in the shoes of a student learning about our discipline for the first time. We cannot take for granted that our charges will be interested in the nuances that now interest us. But we can assume that those paradigm-shifting insights that grabbed us when we were first exposed to them might still grab students today.

Tell students on the first day of class why the course will be important, even crucial, to their lives. As you reach new topics, tell why and how each excites you. Also, simply *tell* them when you reach a point important to the course or to the discipline: "This next concept is critical." How else would they know it's so important?

Moreover, what you do (influencing the next generation; spreading the importance of your discipline) is important, as well as interesting to you. Every class is different; you will learn something new from how your students respond, from what they say.

When you become a good teacher, you will find that serious teaching yields serious rewards. Students may applaud you on the last day of class, even at a school with no tradition of student applause. Some will change their majors just to take another course from you. You will even hear it said about you, sometimes via a third party (which is the best way), "That professor changed my life." You will become a mentor, at least to a few students. For others, with whom you don't share such a major bond, you may still become a role model. That's great! Young adults need adult role models other than their parents.[10]

And here's a perhaps surprising confession: I always *chose* to teach first-year courses. Let me see if I can persuade you to do so, too. First, consider the obvious but often ignored point that dynamic first-year courses entice dynamic students to major in your field. Don't you want dynamic students as majors?[11]

Admittedly, it's interesting and fun to teach higher-level students in seminars that let you explore the cutting edge of your discipline. But it is also interesting and fun—and perhaps more important—to inspire the uninitiated with the key ideas of your discipline. If your discipline has important insights—and it does, does it not, to you at least?—then isn't it worthwhile to share them with as many people as possible?

You also need to participate in getting your department to reward teaching of introductory courses. One way is by giving double teaching credit to faculty members who teach large intro courses with a paired TA seminar. At the same time, the professor needs to develop that seminar into something more than simply a weekly meeting to bring TAs up to date on the mechanics of the course and deal with any problems that have arisen.

In my Introduction to Sociology class, for example, my TAs were involved in developing lessons and assessments that helped them run discussion groups—which operated independently, without my presence—with eight to twelve students. At the end of the semester, for the oral final exam, each of my TAs was responsible for administering a single question to each small group of students taking the test. Each TA discussed with me the participation and learning of each student in the TA's discussion group and in her final exam administration, which aided me in arriving at the semester grades for the class. Through all of this, I delegated some of my responsibility, taught sociology and pedagogy to my TAs, and developed discussion groups that were instructive and active for my students.

Of course, rewarding professors who teach large introductory courses by giving them credit for teaching two courses is paradoxical: On one hand, the department is saying that teaching is valuable, and on the other, it is demonstrating it values teaching by rewarding the avoidance of teaching! A better way is simply to give prestige to the professors who teach large courses. Ask other professors to sit in on their courses occasionally to learn how good teaching is done. The department must mean it when it says it values teaching by giving those professors more money! And this should not exempt chairs or others with administrative responsibilities.

And finally, this: Even if I have not (yet) persuaded you of the value and magic of teaching—even if you still view it as a necessary evil—you will still profit from doing it better. Popular teachers who inspire students find it easier to recruit good students as research assistants. Some inspiring teachers experience the joys of building an empire of student followers and can magnify their impact on the discipline and the world by way of these recruits.

Good Teaching Will Not Wreck Your Life

Even committed professors must limit the time they spend in class, seeing students outside class, grading, and preparing for the next class. The problem is simple: Teaching can be an endless heat sink, absorbing all your professional energies and even sucking energy from your other roles. There always seems to be a class to prepare for, an exam to construct, a student to see, a paper to grade. That's especially true for the novice instructor, who does not already have a course outline or lecture notes to recycle.[12] You must draw a line.

Two "aha" experiences helped me cope with this dilemma. During my first semester of teaching full time at Tougaloo College in Mississippi, I taught three courses that met four times each week. I was single and new to Mississippi that fall, so my social life left me lots of free time. One weekend I spent seventeen hours preparing for my courses. I realized I could not do that every weekend, yet I still had only prepared for Monday's and Tuesday's classes! During the week I was able to prepare more, but when Friday came, I had not prepared for my class in introductory sociology.

I decided to review, so I threw together some obvious questions on the lectures of the first three class periods of the week. To my surprise, the resulting class was the best of the semester to that point. Students struggled to answer my questions, showing me what they had and had not learned. They helped each other with the material. They asked me probing questions that went beyond what I had presented. Neither at Carleton College, where I had done my undergraduate degree, nor at Harvard, where I had earned my doctorate, had I ever experienced a discussion class period in sociology. At both schools, teachers talked while students listened and took notes. Suddenly I saw the value in under preparation! Or, to put it more seriously, I saw the value in taking time to see how the material is "going down"—how it connects with student experiences and preconceptions, and what questions students have that might usefully direct the use of class time.

Two decades later, at the University of Vermont, I was struggling to finish the manuscript for *Lies My Teacher Told Me*. I decided to make Tuesday and Thursday afternoons off-limits for teaching. I shut my previously always-open office door. I did not make up the exam that was due to go out to students following Monday. I did not see students. I did not even answer my phone. Eventually, I finished the book; in the meantime, my teaching did not suffer because I prioritized teaching on days other than Tuesdays and Thursdays. You, too, can balance your teaching, research, writing, family, and influencing the world so none of them suffers.[13]

Plan of the Book

This book is my attempt to get college teachers, future college teachers, and even some high school teachers thinking about ways to communicate better, get students more involved in their subject matter, and do a better job of testing. It is also my swan song as a college teacher. I have taught for half a century and teach no more.[14] This book contains the gimmicks that I used, some of which I developed, which I want to pass on to a new generation of college teachers. It is like that kind of cookbook whose author has tested every recipe. The ideas come from my practice, which has always been informed by experience and by keeping up with the current literature.

You probably have already noticed that I am speaking in the second person here. That is, the book is addressed to "you." I tried writing in the third person: "Good professors will . . ." But "you" seems more direct. I want to speak directly to you. I want to tell you what has worked for me, because I think it may work for you.

Here's what it will cover:

In order to make the ideas about the content of your course that matter to *you* also matter to *your students*, you have to design your course in a way that touches base with what already matters to them—the subject of chapter 1, which offers advice about your syllabus and how to structure the semester.

Chapter 2 focuses on making your course begin with a bang on the first day of class, setting the tone for what is to come. It includes information on how to form a supportive critiquing community in your classroom, and also some thoughts about the fraught topic of trigger warnings.

Chapter 3 covers writing and numeracy. Too many college professors fault students or their high schools for producing graduates who cannot write, create, or understand charts and tables. It falls to us to remedy these woes, not just lament them. You can get students writing, writing well, and understanding a numerical table, even how to set one up themselves. This chapter also offers ideas on assignments that include alternatives to written papers.

In chapter 4, I share my thoughts on how to offer constructive feedback.

Chapter 5, "On (Not) Lecturing," explains why you should expect students to attend your important and interesting classes, and how to structure your courses so that your students do attend! This chapter includes various suggestions on how to get good discussions going in your classroom, discussions that include every student. I'm not at all against lecturing, but this chapter shows how to "curate" your class by including ten-to-twenty-minute lecturettes rather than hour-long lectures. It also gives suggestions about how to use videos and other media and talks about how, when, and why to get students working in groups.

Chapter 6 explains why you should expect students to do your important and interesting reading as the semester goes along, not at its end.

Chapter 7 talks about the importance of testing. It tells why you should test, because testing, properly done, both enhances student learning and gives you a window into what you have taught well and what you must teach better.

Chapter 8 covers *how* to test—an undervalued skill. It also suggests what to do with tests after you give them. Good testing ties in with the objectives of your course and can provide some of the most exciting learning of the semester.

Chapter 9 tackles the tricky topic of grading and evaluation.

Chapter 10 suggests ways to expect and get good performance from a broad, diverse range of students. At least four major student subcultures (collegiate, vocational, intellectual, and nonconformist) exist at almost all higher education institutions. Very different things matter to students of these four types. Understanding them helps you reach each kind of student. I also offer hints on how to make your course important to students from different racial, ethnic, and social class backgrounds than yours, as well as from different age-groups, handicaps, and sexual orientations.

Finally, chapter 11 offers hints for a memorable final day of your course.

Some Last Opening Thoughts

Writing teacher Helen Sword describes how, in her first year of full-time teaching, she "cobbled together courses that looked more or less exactly like the ones I had enrolled in as an undergraduate, and I delivered them in just the same way that they had been delivered to me," even the exams.[15] She observed what her colleagues were doing: not much different. As she recalls, "Not until many years later did I discover that my university library was filled with row upon row of books devoted to topics such as student-centered learning and principles of course design—books that could have helped me . . . had I only known that they existed."[16] That leads to my first suggestion: Read something—anything, even *this* book—about how to teach, how to test, and so on. *Don't* just replicate what was done to you!

This book is as short as I can make it. I don't take much time to prove my statements by citing relevant research. I worry that if I do, you won't read the book. Just start in. If you don't find something useful in the first few pages, then read the first few pages of the chapter on testing—a topic few professors know much about. If you still don't find anything useful, then read a *different* book on teaching. But do read something, as Sword suggests!

Shall we get started?

1

Designing Your Course

At the most general level, you want two things as a college teacher: You want to form your class into a cohesive unit with its own culture, and you want that culture to inspire deep learning. Doing these two things will ensure a good outcome for the semester, in any course. This puts both course planning and first-day impressions—things you have great (if often neglected) control over—at a special premium. In this chapter, I offer my thoughts on how to start on the right foot.

The Bedrock

Both the objectives and the mechanics of any college course should flow from its importance. So, it pays to think hard about this central question: What will students remember from my class in twenty years? How could I design a course to maximize what they retain?

Good answers to this "in twenty years" question might include your own personal passion for the subject. In my case, it was my passion for the subversive aspect of sociology, for the fascinating way it looked underneath the surface. Perhaps they'll remember your course's potential for boosting students' ability to think about the data and methods that underlie the claims of policy studies. Or maybe it will be the class's offering of specific skills, such as statistics, good writing, speaking. It could be you taught them the skills and qualities that help students to do their job as Americans—to bring about the America of the future.

This bedrock reflection is not a one-time occurrence, though! To teach college well, you must apply constant energy to upgrading and fine-tuning your courses so that they comport with such aims and promises and maintain relevancy and interest.

And let me be clear: Teaching is not something that gets in the way of your "real work." Teaching is *at least* as challenging and intellectual as your scholarly research. As you learn what works in the classroom, your students are also showing you how your subject relates or does not relate to American culture and ways of thinking. If you listen to them, they are likely helping you determine what is most important about your discipline. Teaching offers many rewards, including feedback on even your most arcane scholarly topics.

However, the bare minimum of classroom preparation does not suffice. If you do not prepare enough—if you just grab last year's lecture notes the morning of class, make sure you have the right PowerPoint deck for them, and then go off and see students in class but not outside it—you will not realize the intellectual stimulation teaching can provide, and you will devalue teaching even more. But there is a "sweet spot." You need to be familiar with the material and how you want to deliver it. It cannot be recited or droned à la the Ben Stein character in *Ferris Bueller's Day Off.*

Teachers who prepare minimally are more subject to burnout than are teachers who think about their courses and are aware that their students can also teach *them*—if not about the discipline itself, then about how it fits with the students' prior knowledge, what is problematic about it for them, and so on. If you think about this, it becomes obvious. Preparing minimally implies that teaching isn't worth your time. Eventually, you'll have to wonder, "Why am I wasting my time here?" So, the answer to teacher burnout is to teach more, not less, and prepare more, not less.

Thoughts on Syllabi

You want to generate intellectual excitement in your course and in your class meetings. Therefore, you must manifest it! Tell students on the first day of class why the course is important, indeed crucial, to their lives. Tell them this in the syllabus, too. Also tell them why and how it excites *you*. You also want to develop rapport with students. That can start with your engagement. As well, it should begin with your syllabus.

Don't ever be late with your course syllabus. Hand it out the first day. But not just a workmanlike course outline. Is your syllabus fun to read? Does it make you a likable person? *Are* you a likable person? If not, is that because you have assumed that likability is somehow too easy? Or anti-intellectual? Nonsense! You can become likable. At the least, you can fake it! Begin with your syllabus. Its number one purpose is to sell your course.

"Ah, but," you may reply, "I don't *want* more students. I have enough as it is." Or perhaps, "My course is required. I don't *have* to sell it."

That's not the point. You're not handing out your syllabus in the student union, recruiting students with it (although you may be recruiting majors). You're selling your students—already enrolled—on the supreme intellectual importance of your course. You're firing up their enthusiasm: First, to read the entire syllabus; second, to anticipate your course eagerly; and third, to begin building the class into the supportive critiquing group that becomes your partner in learning.

What, then, is the syllabus? In addition to laying out the content matter that will be covered, it is a document that states and maps out what they, as college students, must accomplish:

—Keep current with the reading.
—Keep current with course assignments.
—Study with other students on occasion.
—Seek assistance in class by asking good questions.
—Seek assistance outside class from you or TAs.
—Participate in discussion.
—Use the syllabus.
—Review for exams.

Design your syllabus and every class meeting to ensure these things happen. Above all, you must keep students from disengaging in the first part of the semester. Once they are accustomed to doing something for your course every single class meeting, it will become a habit.

So, how can we do that?

The first sentence of your syllabus should tell students who the intended audience for the course is, and why it's important for that specific audience. If your course is introductory or general, then presumably it's important for all humankind, right? Don't be shy; make that claim, but only as a hook. (You will make a more refined version of it at greater length a little later in the book.)

The rest of your first paragraph should do what the first paragraph of a good speech usually does: Tell your audience what you are going to say, say it, then reiterate what you said. There are other ways to set up a good introduction, but that advice is sound. So, this first paragraph should give students a quick overview of what the course is going to "say."

Here is the first paragraph from the syllabus for a course I taught repeatedly at the University of Vermont (UVM):

> Race Relations in the United States is particularly intended for nonmajors at the University of Vermont who have not had a prior course in sociology. Too often, Americans think racism is abnormal, an aberration, something to be explained psychologically. To put racism in a social structural rather than psychological perspective, and to get students thinking about what causes racism to increase and decrease over time, the course opens with a considerable treatment of slavery. We begin with chunks of *Gone with the Wind*, partly because this book and movie have so dominated American culture. Then we read chunks of Margaret Walker's *Jubilee*, often called a "Black *Gone with the Wind*." Students now have two opposite views of slavery, the Civil War, and Reconstruction, which raises important issues of how we know things in society. Additional sources will help you decide.

The above paragraph introduced only the first two weeks of the course; I used another paragraph to cover the rest, with the aim of being dramatic and informative, not comprehensive. I wanted the syllabus to excite students and also give them an overview of what to expect. The second paragraph began, "Race relations is not only a matter of black and white, of course. Indeed, race relations in this hemisphere began with Columbus." This segue tells students to expect coverage of Native Americans, later Chinese Americans, Mexican Americans, and so on. Finally, the second paragraph claims that the course will help students see and understand the role of race relations in society today and give them ideas about how to improve race relations tomorrow.

Of course, your syllabus will be different from mine. Your first paragraph or two will foretell what *your* course will do. But surely your course has drama too, even if it is in accounting or biochemistry. (Incidentally, I mean no disrespect to accounting, biochemistry, or any other field. I took a chemistry course that was "pitched" with drama, including in its course syllabus, and another that wasn't, and I still feel gratified that I completed the first, while I dropped the second halfway through.) Give your outline a narrative arc. If your course has no storyline, no excitement, why are you teaching it? If it has, then show your students that arc and let them in on that excitement from the very beginning of the course syllabus.

Make the argument in your syllabus for why the course is important and interesting to people apart from the usual suspects. Maybe you argue it's essential to all of society! To be sure, a course required for a student's major is important by definition. Students majoring in business administration may be required to take a course in accounting. Students in nursing at UVM had to take my race relations course. You don't want to settle for the mere fact of the requirement, however. The requirement puts warm bodies in your classroom (at least on the first day of class), but you want *excited* warm bodies.

You can also tie your course to the broader intellectual issues it relates to. The critical question you must ask yourself as you plan your course and as you write your syllabus is: How do you want students to have changed when they leave your course three or four months from now? Once you have figured this out, your conclusions will inform everything you do in the course, most especially your syllabus. Do not hide your conclusions. Place them boldly right here in your syllabus, so students know exactly why they're taking the course.

Another option might be to include a passage by some luminary that lays out the field and its allure. On the first page of my introductory sociology syllabus, I inserted an entire paragraph modified slightly from the first chapter of *The Sociological Imagination*, by the well-known sociologist C. Wright Mills, author of *The Power Elite*. Since I am *still* passionate about sociology, I'm going to include it here for you, even though you may be a professor of physics or poetry:

> Nowadays people often feel that their private lives are a series of traps. They sense that within their everyday worlds, they cannot quite overcome their troubles, and in this feeling, they are often quite correct. Yet people do not usually define the troubles they endure in terms of historical change and institutional contradiction. They do not possess the quality of mind essential to grasp the interplay of man and society, of biography and history. What people need, and what they feel they need, is a quality of mind that will help them to use information and to develop reason in order to understand what is going on in the world and what may be happening within themselves. It is this quality of mind . . . that may be called the sociological imagination.[1]

You might reasonably respond to this passage by observing that lots of people do *not* feel that their private lives are a series of traps. College students on the cusp of their adult lives may not feel that to be true, especially if they come from affluent families. But I spent the bulk of my teaching career at one of the most affluent universities in the United States (in terms of students' family income), so I can attest that Mills's insight is a good sociological observation. I responded to it in my course syllabus by going on to say:

> Those "on top of" society, I might add, those in its upper and upper-middle classes, often do *not* feel trapped or even directed by social structure. But they are. Their very unawareness itself results from their position in social structure.

With those two paragraphs, I hoped to have sucked in my students, even those taking the course because it was required in nursing, or was recommended in forestry, or met at a convenient hour. At least I gave it a shot.

Another alternative is to show students why other professors in your field consider your course central to the major, or why professors in other fields consider it important to those fields. If another field requires its students to take your course, ask a professor in that department to tell you why.

Perhaps there are different ways you can describe your course to make it important to different students. Considering your college's main student subcultures is often a good idea. Students in, say, the vocational subculture—perhaps attending college mainly to get certified as a registered nurse—will have different reasons for valuing your course than students in the intellectual subculture. Or your course may be relevant to students' other interests, to their own interior growth, to issues in which they may or should be interested, or indeed, to the state of the nation or the world. At the University of Vermont, for example, my race relations syllabus used two paragraphs to argue for the importance of the course. The first was local:

> Perhaps at this university, this semester, no argument need be made regarding the importance of race relations. The University of Vermont has seen a series of major race relations events. [I then shared some of the highlights of racial incidents at the school, including those that occurred in the previous semester.]

The second paragraph cited national and international events of the previous year. "The subject matter of this course continues to be a central issue in our society," I concluded. (Sadly, and urgently, this sentence continues to hold just as true as ever, if not more so.)

Since your course *is* important, you can conclude, it is vital that students come to class, participate in class, and hear the reactions from other students and the professor, as part of the learning process. It thus follows, the introduction to your syllabus can forewarn, that students who sign on for the course are agreeing to take it seriously, do the reading *before* it is supposed to be discussed, talk in class, and put in a great deal of work.

Those last four words then can furnish a segue to a later section of the syllabus, "Course Requirements." First, however, you need to tell students what you want them to know and be able to do as a result of taking your course.

Be clear: Expect attendance. If you teach at a community college or commuter college where most students also have outside jobs, add the phrase "as you do at your job." Expect students to be on time. Expect discussion participation. Say so. Expect group work. Say so. Expect respect for you and for other students. Say so. You are building a team, or maybe a bunch of teams (study groups, project groups, sections). Ask students to see you immediately if one or more of these expectations is beyond their power. They won't, but by not seeing you, they have "bought into" the expectations. Also ask them to see you immediately if they have any learning disability, such as one that requires special testing circumstances. Read these requirements aloud so everyone is clear on them. Students may not be late, either, and should send an explanation ahead of time if they're going to be late or must leave during class. Say so.

As a matter of overall goals and bottom-line expectations, tell students that you are ultimately asking them to form a "supportive critiquing community." If they feel they cannot do so, they will want to take a different course. You reserve the right to drop students who misbehave, and you should say so on the first day of class and in your syllabus. The preceding sounds punitive, but I don't mean it that way—and you shouldn't either. Gently mention some of the topics you think might be problematic for some students to hear about—racism, for example, violence, maybe a video of a graphic medical operation. Invite students to visit you in your office or after class "today" (that first day of class) if they wish. Otherwise, point out that their taking the course amounts to a form of contract in which they, by staying, assent to its substance and agree to be supportive and critiquing.

Consider adding extra credit tasks designed to get students to try things they may not have thought about before: visiting the writing center with their research papers, obtaining a source through interlibrary loan, or conducting an interview.

Allow students to drop one requirement (perhaps *not* including the final). This can be automatic: *You* will drop their worst grade (perhaps not including the final). I used this idea to get buy-in from my own children when they were growing up. When chores were to be done around the house, I would make up the list of necessary tasks, and my children and I would discuss them. I would allow them to assign one of the chores to me with the theory that by having them also be in a position of power, they wouldn't feel powerless and less likely to engage in the chores system. The same principle holds true with the idea of giving students the power to identify which assignment will not be a part of their assessment. If you want a collective decision, you could allow students to vote on which item is to be dropped. It could spark an interesting discussion among students arguing for various alternatives.

If there is a research paper or project component to your course, have students put their papers up on the web, especially if you can come up with a focus and title for that part of your course. This larger audience prompts them to do a better job. For that matter, there's nothing wrong with a poster session. You can invite other faculty members and/or senior students to judge or comment on the displays.

Finally, never forget the power of variety. It's important at several levels, including as a tool for dealing with the inevitable waxing and waning of energy and interest across academic terms. You'll want to capitalize on openings and counteract doldrums. On this front, I've found that Donna K. Duffy and Janet W. Jones's book *Teaching Within the Rhythms of the Semester* helps me work out smart plans and schemes.[2] So, look around. Some excellent scholars are thinking about such things, and it's helpful to stay abreast of their debates and findings.

The Rhythm of the Semester

Most teachers demand more actual work from students toward the end of the semester. They may not realize they are doing so. They may require lots of reading in the first eight weeks of their course, for example, but that reading may not happen. If they require a paper or major project, almost surely, it's due near the end of the semester. The final exam comes at the end of the semester, of course.

This doesn't work. Even if your students have the best of intentions, even if they like your course, even if they are excited about their paper topic or project, toward the end of the semester they face multiple deadlines. They may have to give priority to another course, especially one that they have *not* enjoyed, simply because they are so far behind in it.

You want to trick them. You want to get more work—good work, exciting learning—from them. To do so, set up early deadlines. Pile up work in the first third of the course, before other courses have done so. This, of course, will be unpopular, but I've found that you can turn this to your advantage. Do so by inviting student input on deadlines! Explain the front-load idea. Invite input on "laddering" deadlines (see below) for papers. Lay out the logic and benefits of front-loading college courses. If you give them the chance, students do see the point of getting their tuition's worth.

Of course, one way students might still react to what they see as an overwhelming workload is to cut corners. They might not do the work at all. They might do shoddy work, turning in a paper bleary-eyed after an all-nighter. They may even rely on the work of someone else, either intentionally or unintentionally. To lessen the likelihood of any of this happening, you need to acknowledge all of these possibilities in your teaching.

First off, be clear in your course outline about what plagiarism is and why it matters. On the first day of class, discuss plagiarism.[3] Note that there are two kinds. There are going to be students who don't understand the rules about using quotation marks and footnotes. Go over those rules. Basically, there are two: If you quote, use quotation marks and footnote. If you "merely" use someone's ideas, footnote.

The second kind of plagiarism is different. It entails trying to get credit for work that is not the student's own. This requires a basic conversation. This kind of student does not understand the purpose of life! Why would she spend thousands of her family's dollars to forge a credential? Does she think the workplace wants people with forged credentials? Would she want to have her teeth worked on by someone who passed dental school without really learning and doing the work?

For the rest of your life, people will expect that you, as a college graduate, know some things, have thought about some things, have read some things. If you avoid those things, then you will be a fraud. From time to time, you may get found out. Even if you don't, you may worry about it. After all, the world is *not* a game. People really *do* do things in life. Teddy Roosevelt put it this way: "Far and away the best prize that life has to offer is the chance to work hard at work worth doing." Maybe your purpose in teaching is to help students prepare to do work worth doing. *Tell* students that! Once they understand, games like plagiarism become beside the point. You may also want to tell them that if this course seems "Mickey Mouse" and worthless—if they are not interested in learning the stuff that it is about—then they should get out of it and take something that *does* interest them.

Pro Tip: Avoid a Punitive Syllabus

Many—most?—professors have a suspicion lurking about in the interior of their brains that students, at least some of them, are trying to get away with something. Of course, some students *are* trying to get away with something—the least amount of work they can do and still get an A-minus, or whatever they consider their target grade. That's called beating the system. It's the extreme version of the student side in the reigning compact of complacency. For you to give in to that mindset is a mistake, for several reasons.

First, assuming that students are *not* sincerely interested in learning can become a self-fulfilling prophecy. When I guest speak at colleges, I always encourage the opposite assumption: I suggest to my hosts that after my campus-wide talk, they hold a book signing. I do so to encourage the intellectual subculture on campus. I point out that the campus store orders the books on consignment and can return them at no cost if they don't sell. Then, in my talk, I reference the sale and suggest to whom the students might give the book—their parents maybe, or a high school teacher—after they finish reading it. I know and admit to my hosts that most students will not buy the book (although sometimes they do sell out). Even if only a few copies are sold, the event is not a failure, because for at least a moment, students have found themselves in a group that is *expected* to buy a book, or at least to consider doing so. In itself, that is a good thing; someday maybe they'll actually buy a book not required for a class.

Conversely, to the degree that your casual remarks in class or your syllabus policies convey to students that you consider them members of a group that is expected to try to beat the system, you increase the chances that they will conceive of themselves the same way. That can only *dis*courage the intellectual subculture on campus. After all, most students do what they think most students do. If they go to Swarthmore, where they think most students study, they study. If they go to the University of Colorado, where they think most students party, they party.

Second, the assumption that students aren't interested in learning disrespects them. More than half a century later, I still recall my disgust at Harvard for the way adminstrators tested graduate students at the end of our first semester. They placed the fifty-five of us taking the introductory graduate course in social relations in Memorial Hall, a huge auditorium, rather than our regular classroom. Then they had us sit in every third seat in every third row. Then they mixed us in with students from several other courses in the rows between. I still remember that they placed Sanskrit students in the rows ahead of us, so even if we were so desperate as to copy from students' answers in another discipline, we couldn't; even the alphabet was different! Not one professor sat in the room, so if students could not understand a question, even one with a misprint, they had no recourse. Only proctors were there, ensuring we did not cheat. The arrangements implied that the intellectual subculture was not to be found among graduate students at Harvard; what existed was only cheating that had to be policed.

Third, assuming students are trying to get away with something can lead to bad teaching. Cynicism has a strong tendency to undermine the kind of creativity, effort, and willful optimism that has always marked great teaching. Don't give it air.

Finally, if you assume that students are not just trying to beat the system but instead to *game* it—that is, to get a good grade *without* doing the work—you will never learn about their occasional real problems, which they need to be able to bring to you. The way you write your syllabus, or the way you present it on the first day of class, can send this message. Then students who face real challenges, either from your material and methods or from some crisis in their personal lives, will avoid seeing you, afraid you'll infer they're just trying to avoid doing the work.

Certainly, you want to be firm. You do students no favor by handing out incompletes like restaurateurs giving out coupons in Times Square; students only wind up falling behind in the next semester while finishing up the old one. Your syllabus needs serious deadlines, including deadlines for the smaller steps necessary for a large project—a proposal, an outline, a bibliography, a draft, and a final draft perhaps, which I call "laddering." But you need to say, with sincerity, "*Please* come see me if you find yourself falling behind in the course. *Please* see me if some serious personal matter is interfering with your performance." You want to be tough but engaging. Students don't want an easy professor. That's not whom they remember decades later.

Course Calendar

Usually, I provide a complete daily calendar for the course in the syllabus, with the note "subject to revision." I preface each new unit with a paragraph introducing it or explaining what is most important about the topic. Way back in the recesses of their brains, many professors think that students should figure out for themselves what are the most important ideas of a course or in a field. Simply telling them, the common thought goes, is spoon-feeding them. Then we give them bad grades when they don't know the most important ideas of a course. I say "we" because I've been afflicted by this mindset myself, once or twice. Don't succumb! If a student were to combine the paragraphs that introduce each unit, they would then have a useful summary of the important points in the course.

A syllabus should provide an intellectual outline of the subject matter of the course. Usually, the chronological presentation of the topic will also be the logical presentation of the topic. That is, your course will flow logically, teaching students the things they need to understand first, first. Hence, your course calendar will also be a logical outline of the material. Point this out! I do it by imposing a formal structure on the calendar. Thus, the introduction is preceded by the Roman numeral I, and covering that information may take two class meetings. The first topic will be preceded by the Roman numeral II. (let's say "Slavery" if I'm teaching race relations) and may take three classes. Don't hide the structure behind the daily calendar. Students need both at once.

You can also make your syllabus a tool that is useful long after the course ends by outlining the essential literature. Include a paragraph that introduces students to the new unit, and make sure to refer to your syllabus when you start any new unit. You might include a quotation, maybe from one of the readings in the unit, that presages what you want students to think about in the unit or encapsulates what you want them to take from it. You can build your syllabus into your class by asking students to read the quote or the introductory paragraph and react to it, perhaps with a question or a summary. Or suggest that students come up with their own goals for taking the course. Make that the subject of their first required journal entry. Now you're well launched!

As you create your course schedule, don't just list content topics. Consider what kind of learning you want students to do, what kinds of skills you want them to build, and how you will teach each topic.

Bear in mind that your syllabus is a contract, and you must uphold your end of it. You may make changes in your schedule, but you should minimize them and announce them clearly. You may not make changes that increase the load on students. You may delete an assignment, but you may not add one.

If you assign reading, use it in some way in class or explain to students how they can use it. Students feel cheated or fooled if they read something and then it doesn't get used. The reference to the reading doesn't have to be elaborate; it can be as simple as talking for a moment in class about what's so great about it and inviting students to chime in. Be sure to tell students to finish the assigned reading before each class, so they will be able to participate effectively. And one cardinal rule: Don't assign an expensive textbook and then barely use it.

Timely work is important for both you and the students. Expect papers and projects to be on time, and get students' graded work back to them ASAP. I try to do so at the very next class period. Why? Because one of the reasons I assign papers is to get a sense of students' understandings and views and, where needed, correct or critique them. Sometimes this critique should be done en masse—after a majority of students have missed the same important point, for example. The student with the late paper cannot really participate in this discussion meaningfully, because they haven't yet written the paper. The paper then becomes a "dead letter"; there's little point in your reading or grading it after such a discussion. So, I make it clear to students that this is the reason I take off credit for late papers.

Require a conference with each student in your office at least once in the semester, preferably early. Maybe again later, especially if any long-term assignment (such as a project or paper) looms.

The most important part of the course outline is a section titled "To Do for Next Class." Don't just assign a reading; assign a task to accompany it, such as coming up with a specific question about a part of the reading. Students might also be asked to meet with the student they've been paired with and read each other's papers or write a journal entry about a reading.

Include in your syllabus any campus resources that you think at least some students will find useful. For instance, if you will use the U.S. Census, include the location of government documents on your campus and the name of a librarian who particularly knows them. If your course involves writing (and I hope most do), include the location of the writing center, if your campus has one, and perhaps the name of a particularly helpful staff person there.

Halfway through the semester, request feedback, perhaps handing out a very simple three-item form:

—What you liked so far about this course
—What you *dis*liked so far about this course
—Your suggestions for the rest of the semester

As you read through the questionnaire responses, keep in mind that it's not too late to drop a reading (so as to better concentrate on others, or to catch up on your syllabus). It's not too late to scaffold a major project better. It's not too late to change your classroom routine if your classroom routine is too routine.

By the way, I do have a rationale for my practice of letting students drop one grade. As biologist James Zull has written in *The Art of Changing the Brain*, "One important rule for helping people learn is to help the learner feel she is in control." Susan A. Ambrose et al.'s *How Learning Works: Seven Research-Based Principles for Smart Teaching* argues that mastery arises when we "allow students to choose among options and make choices that are consistent with their goals and the activities that they value." So, by giving students choices over certain avenues to their goals, I am hoping to help them value the learning and the class even more.

Include in your syllabus the requirement that students bring your syllabus to class every day. It's easy to incorporate it into their notebook. (And do emphasize that students should take notes physically, on paper. Research shows that such note-taking results in more learning than taking notes on screen or not taking notes at all.) Refer to the syllabus in almost every class period, asking students to review the assignment for next time in class, for instance. I like to begin a new unit with a quotation by someone famous or a memorable introduction that sets the tone—and advise that students need to see it and read it, not just hear it, in class.

Leave lots of white space in your syllabus. You should use your own master hard copy to write notes every class period as to what worked, what didn't, what changes to make for next class, what changes to make for next year. Your students will use the white space to note changes (because a syllabus is a living, growing, changing document), crucial points, summarize a reading or an entire unit, and so forth.

Within your syllabus, perhaps just before the class schedule, insert a request to email you something fun related to the course—maybe an image from the web that illustrates an important concept that you'll discuss in the second or third class. Tell students what to put as the subject of their email. Make it due before the second or third class. Give students a bonus point (or more) for doing so. Then you'll know who has read the syllabus, and you can send an email to those who did not respond, reminding them to read the syllabus.

If your college has a page or more of boilerplate guidelines that must be given out in every course, do not let that interfere with the important educational tasks that your syllabus plays. Your syllabus cannot play any constructive role unless students read it. If your college requires including such a boilerplate document, make it an appendix, reference it in your syllabus, and hand it out separately.

That said, you should read the boilerplate and take it seriously. Many of its guidelines may stem from important considerations or unfortunate past incidents or practices. Encourage students to read them, and if there are any items that you deem important to your course, incorporate them into your syllabus. For example, the college may require that students be told of the existence and role of the campus counseling office, standards on cheating and plagiarism, or college policy on absences. Those things should be in your syllabus. This is also where I discuss other regulations a professor should (and sometimes must) follow. If a student tells you they are suicidal, you need to report that, and you need to be open about explaining that you will do so. Same for assault.

Construct your syllabus to be your friend in case a student tries to argue (to you or to your chair or dean) that you have been unfair to her. With such clarity in your syllabus, you can more easily explain that giving a paper a B, which may be 85 in your system, doesn't mean she "lost" 15 points. It means she earned a B. Also, avoid the phrasing I just used—that you "gave" a B. She earned a B. The attention should be on her, her work, her choice, and what she can do to earn a higher grade, not on you and why you "gave" her a "lower" one.

Ask students who have an issue with a grade to do two things: (1) share the issue with one other student to see if another student in the course agrees that the grade is unfair, and (2) come see you in your office the next day (or soon thereafter). This gets them talking and also in your door, which is what you want and where you want them in general. Good things can happen one-on-one; use any excuse to reach out, encourage peer discussion, and get them coming to see you outside of class!

2

The First Day of Class

It's part of the culture at some universities for many professors to write off the first day of class. They have good reason, as it's not until the second class or even later that the class roster is settled. Various factors cause student turnover—incomplete registration, advising still in process, late arrivals, dropped courses elsewhere in the college. As a result, students may be adding courses for a week or more without even being thought of as latecomers. Professors conclude that whatever content they teach on opening day they'll merely have to repeat later. Responding to this problem by using the first day to do some clerical tasks and distribute the syllabus sets a terrible precedent, however. Philosophically, it implies that you don't care if problems interfere with your course content. But you do! Your course is important, both to you and to students.

Luckily, a simple solution is available: make a video recording of the first day of class. Require students who join your course after the first day to watch it. Post it online for students to watch.[1] Announce this to all students, including those who are present on opening day, for it implies to them that every class is important, and you therefore expect them to come to every one.

On the first day, be sure to get to class early. Talk with students in the corridor outside. Some will have questions about the course. If none does, ask them about themselves. Pull out your enrollment list and even jot down notes to help you begin to differentiate your students and learn about them. Also, ask why they are taking the course.

As soon as you can get into your room, put up an outline of what you plan to do that day on the blackboard (or whiteboard). (See chapter 5, "On [Not] Lecturing," for a discussion of what goes into such an outline.) You should do this every class. Then spend the final minutes before your class is scheduled to start by talking with early-comers. I suggest you go to the back of the room and engage a couple of students sitting next to each other in conversation. Again, jot down notes. If you don't want students sitting in the way back, invite them to move up. One by one they'll assent.

Start your first class on time, even though students may still be meandering in. Inform the class that you will *always* start on time. Invite students to be there *ahead* of time to meet with you; pledge to be there at least five minutes early. If you have TAs, station one outside the open door the first day (but within earshot) to hand out the course outline to latecomers and orient them to whatever activity is now going on inside. Ask that TA to emphasize to the latecomers that they be on time from then on. If you don't have a TA, put a pile of course outlines on a desk just inside the door and ask a student seated nearby to draw it to the attention of latecomers.

Start with the basics. Note that you require attendance and will occasionally take attendance. To emphasize the necessity of engagement in the class, take attendance and record participation. Early in the semester, meet with students who are silent in class, who are reported by your TAs as problematic in some way, who get a D or F on the first exam, who are absent more than once, and so on. Tell them you expect them to come, and you expect to hear from them, and you expect better performance on the next exam. Suggest they write down a question or comment about the class material at home, then they can read it in class to intitiate or engage in a discussion.

Trust your students. Expect a lot from them.[2] Tell them you expect them to do well. They need to believe this *in order to* do well. This is especially true when learning hard things, or areas that students consider hard, such as statistics in sociology.

If students think they are likely to fail, they may not try hard because it's better for their self-esteem to fail through lack of effort than through lack of ability.[3] They'd rather be thought of (and think of themselves) as lazy than stupid. Of course, if they are lazy, they won't learn it, but if they try, they might, so we must get them to try!

Expect students to buy the readings, unless they are available online or in other ways. Don't allow pleadings of poverty. Be respectful of student budgets when you choose your readings, but then encourage them to buy the books and read them. Explain why owning books matters, even (or perhaps especially) in our new era. Physical books do not only facilitate superior reading outcomes; having them around also increases the chances of returning to wells of knowledge, insight, and inspiration. Additionally, printed books bolster a whole ecosystem of writers, librarians, and small shopkeepers. They also show your own kids and friends that you are a lifelong learner, while making it tangibly possible to pay this forward. In a later chapter, I explain even further the reasons why owning books is important to college students.

The First Five Minutes

We have all heard speakers (including at religious services) routinely say "Good morning" (or "Good afternoon" or "Good evening") as a way to begin their talk. We've also heard them say it in a way that means it and commands and gets a reply. Say it that way. If silence ensues, say, "Wait a minute, you can do better than that—good *morning*!" That wakes them up and gets them participating, even if only minimally, at the start of the class period. You can decide if you want to repeat that custom every class thereafter. The important thing is immediately to create an atmosphere in your first class, and then in each subsequent class meeting, that is hospitable, conducive to students' feeling comfortable and safe to participate, and professional, conveying that important education is about to take place.

For the first day, do not invent some stupid icebreaker. The questions you ask the first day should tie directly to the course and the syllabus. A terrific way to learn what students know (and think they know) is to ask them to generate estimates of basic facts relevant to your discipline. Who knows what you will learn from the answers they might give you? If you are able to access the results instantly, you can have an outstanding teachable moment immediately! Learn when they think the modernism era occurred, or how many chromosomes they think most people have. You can also ask students to answer questions relevant to their understanding of their world. Perhaps a literature professor asks what their favorite poem is and why. Or an economics professor asks about the ways inflation appears in students' lives. A significant moment for me occurred when I asked my Sociology of Race Relations students at the University of Vermont to guess the racial composition of the United States. and received from them absurdly high estimates of Black people's share of the population.

Or the opening activity can entail asking students what they already know about the subject matter, either of the entire course or of that first day. You may learn something astounding: An "aha" moment way back in 1969 convinced me of the importance of learning about what students think they know. I was teaching at Tougaloo College in Mississippi. I asked my freshman seminar on the first day of class, "What happened during Reconstruction?" Sixteen of my seventeen students, all African Americans, replied something along the lines of: That was the period right after the Civil War when Blacks took over the government of the Southern states, but they were too soon out of slavery, so they screwed up, and whites had to take control again.

I sat stunned. At least three lies resided in that sentence. First, African Americans never "took over." During Reconstruction, all Southern states had white governors, and all but one had white legislative majorities. Second, the Reconstruction governments did *not* "screw up." The excellent state constitutions written during the Reconstruction upheld the 13th, 14th, and 15th amendments; guaranteeing freedom, property rights, and voting rights to Black as well as white citizens; started public schools for African Americans; and passed many other beneficial measures. Finally, it wasn't whites in general who took control in the backlash against Reconstruction. It was specifically white supremacist Democrats—indeed, it was the original Ku Klux Klan.

I visited nearby high schools and watched teachers uncritically presenting inaccurate material on Reconstruction in textbooks written during the pre–civil rights era. Then I understood. My students had simply learned what they had been taught. This convinced me that history had been deployed as a weapon against my students. To some extent, it still is. Therefore, teachers need to give students weapons to use in self-defense. By learning about my students, I gained an opportunity to focus lessons, cover blind spots, and engage with students on the importance of sociology right away.

I often hand out a questionnaire on the first day of class, though the questions differ depending on the course. If you choose to do this, include some questions about the basic insights of your discipline, whatever it is. You never know what students know (and what they *don't* know) until they tell you. An arresting example occurred to me when I did this in the fall semester of 1993 as I was trying to finish my book *Lies My Teacher Told Me*. I decided to teach a course with that same title; its subtitle was "Issues in Secondary Social Studies Education." That way I could hand out some of my chapters and get feedback; I could also get students involved in wrestling with some of the issues.

Perhaps owing to its flamboyant title, the seminar was oversubscribed. I wound up with more than forty students—mostly juniors and seniors majoring in history, the social sciences, and education.

On the first day of class, I gave out a quiz. I often do this, seeking to learn more about what my students know and don't know. One question asked, "The War in Vietnam was fought between _____ and _____." I wanted to see how many students replied with "between North and South Vietnam" compared with "between the United States and Vietnam." To my consternation, 22 percent of my students replied with "between North and South Korea!"

Another exercise, which I often used in my Intro to Sociology class, was having students create a budget for someone who works in the laundry at a nearby hospital. Beforehand, I would phone the nearest large hospital to learn what it pays its laundry staff. Next, I would scour the "furnished apartments" classifieds and note the second-cheapest, reasonably located offering. Finally, I'd check the rates for two children, ages two and four, at a daycare center.

Then, I'd tell the class to engage in an exercise of imaginative empathy: How much did they think a member of the laundry staff was paid? And how would they spend their money if they were a single laundry worker with two small children?

At this point, I would challenge them: You balance it. They can try—eliminate the apartment's phone and its monthly costs, incorporate government funding, if available—and they see it's impossible. This person cannot afford to work! If she is at home taking care of the kids, then there is no need to buy work uniforms or half as many other clothes and shoes. There is no bus fare or childcare. But if she doesn't work, she cannot afford new clothes or any of life's pleasures: going to the movies or the occasional outing. She misses the rent once in a while because, whether on welfare or working a job, she is receiving perhaps 74 percent of a viable budget. And what is the answer? Job training? A better job? Is it not clear that the hospital makes her poor? Students see this in action, they engage with it and try to solve it, and this means they are taking the topic seriously.

Sometimes I hand out some of those same questions again near the end of the course and ask students to ruminate on the differences in their replies. Hopefully, there are some! Consider ending the course by having them write a letter to their former selves, explaining what they now know.

By starting the first class in this fashion, you have established the tenor of the semester for the students. According to Professor Cathy N.

Davidson, "Most students have no idea what they are supposed to be learning in a classroom beyond the 'content' level, nor do they know why the content is valid in and of itself nor what use or application or purpose it will have beyond the final exam."[4] You do not want your students to feel this way. You want them prepped from the first day to be thinking about what the course is for and what they can do with its content, and, by the end, for them to be competent enough to use it moving forward in their classes and their lives.

Generally, students need to have something to do the first minute they come in and sit down. Otherwise, bored, they will turn on their phones or laptops and go elsewhere (the web, videos, emails, talking with friends, etc.). Then you will have to *drag* them back to the classroom to get their attention, interrupting what may (by then) be an important activity.

One idea is to put the first question you're going to ask them onscreen or on the board as soon as class starts. Or you can use the time for them to ask you questions.

Or, another easy and useful way to engage students: When you hand out the syllabus, have them read it and come up with a question. Then, pair them up and have each pair decide on their best question to ask. The question can also be about something *not* on the syllabus.

Trigger Warnings, Also Known as "Heads-Ups"

Put a trigger warning in your course syllabus if there is a substantial chance that you or your students will discuss anything that might cause anyone serious anxiety. I suspect many college courses will discuss something that might do this. (Maybe math, but probably not.) Read the trigger warning aloud on the first day of class. Embed it in your "supportive critiquing community" discussion. That is, explain that while you do this out of respect for any members of the community who need it, this is not a license to avoid the difficult topic. Invite students who feel they need to discuss a possible problem to do so with you in your office.

After that is taken care of, please be aware that college *should* trigger some kinds of anxiety. Rethinking one's positions can trigger anxiety, and higher education *should* prompt rethinking of one's positions—about race, for example. About sexual orientation as a topic, and sometimes even about one's own orientation. About patriotism versus nationalism. About religions, and sometimes even about one's own. Such rethinking is discomfiting and *should* be. However, trigger warnings exist for a reason. The serious reaction of a person suffering PTSD due to a traumatic experience is a different matter than mere anxiety. Some people with PTSD may seek (and merit) a dispensation to avoid a certain reading, video, or entire topic. However, no student should be allowed to avoid a topic simply because of worry or discomfort. They are adults, after all, and cannot avoid topics that exist in the real world. A trigger warning does not excuse students from material. Quite the contrary, it asks them to prepare themselves for a tough topic so they can manage their emotions and handle it successfully.

As Barbara Jones, the executive director of the Freedom to Read Foundation, has said, "Avoiding a topic does not make it go away. In fact, engaging in uncomfortable content, at college, where one is surrounded by peers and support groups, is the best way."[5] High school teachers often avoid discussing social class, racism, and other topics, deeming them too hot—and indeed, some states have recently legislated prohibitions on materials that "include or promote . . . discomfort, guilt, anguish, or another form of psychological distress" due to "race or sex."[6] Such proscription in persons of a different group or race—but that does not make such topics go away. Indeed, it may increase their power.

I do not mean to trivialize or oversimplify any of this. I do, however, agree with the American Association of University Professors, which, in a 2014 statement approved by its Committee on Academic Freedom and Tenure, concluded:

> The presumption that students need to be protected rather than challenged in a classroom is at once infantilizing and anti-intellectual. It makes comfort a higher priority than intellectual engagement. . . . Of course, there may be instances in which a teacher judges it necessary to alert students to potentially difficult material and that is his or her right. Administrative requirements are different from individual faculty decisions. . . . Trigger warnings thus run the risk of reducing complex literary, historical, sociological and political insights to a few negative characterizations. By calling attention to certain content in a given work, trigger warnings also signal an expected response to the content (e.g., dismay, distress, disapproval), and eliminate the element of surprise and spontaneity that can enrich the reading experience and provide critical insight.[7]

In a way, a trigger warning is like a spoiler alert. It warns the audience member or reader that something is coming up that requires care. Trigger warnings do not exempt students from watching a distressing movie; they help students watch that movie *better*. Trigger warnings do not excuse students from participating in a wrenching discussion; they help students contribute to it. Once in a while, however, you may need to give an alternative assignment.

It's also important to distinguish between feeling bad and PTSD. I recall a question I got in a public forum from the parent of a student at Wellesley High School in Massachusetts. He complained that his now-adult daughter was subjected to a weeklong unit on the Holocaust, including videos, and she "came home at the end of it in tears." I replied, first, by asking him, "How old is your daughter now?"

He replied, "Thirty-five."

"Have you ever talked with her about that lesson since her high school days?"

He said he had not.

"Have that conversation," I suggested. "I bet, when you do, that she will remember that unit, and I suspect she *won't* recall lots of other units that she experienced that year."

He allowed that I was probably correct about that. I went on to say that I saw nothing wrong about coming home in tears from a unit on the Holocaust—that was a healthy reaction. We should not protect high school students from a unit on the Holocaust. After all, we do want them to know about the Holocaust, do we not? Consider that only one in six Americans ever takes a course in history after leaving high school. If they don't get it in high school, when *will* they get it? And surely, we want them to encounter the facts and immorality of the Holocaust in an organized setting, with the aid of a dedicated teacher.

I suggest that no topic we think is important for people to think about should be off-limits to college discussion. Your syllabus should include suggestions on what students might *do* when they are upset with some aspect of your course, whether over a video, reading, comment by you, or the reaction of a fellow student. Usually, the first step is to arrange to see you. Encourage this and note that they do not have to wait for your next scheduled office hour. When they arrive, you owe them a serious and empathetic hearing. A second suggestion is to ask them to make use of the college counseling service. Before the semester ends, a student can visit and meet with at least one counselor. If they seem open to this, then recommend the counselor by name.

Start building such care and resilience on this first day. In this, I have found the phrase "supportive critiquing community" to be useful in achieving such cohesion. Since you have already established (or at least asserted) that your topic is important, it follows that you need to form a supportive critiquing community to master it. All three words are important. You want students to make new friends and establish what Stanford sociologist Mark Granovetter calls "weak ties" in your classroom. Your common goal: learning about this (important!) subject and how it is meaningful to you, personally. We want all students to do well in this course. (I typically announce that I'm a tough grader, but that in the past, most students have done well.) You might invite alumni of the course who liked it to speak on the first day.

This moment is a great time to hold a discussion on how to form such a supportive critiquing community.

Ask the students to ponder the educational and ethical value of a reasonable amount of reasonable discomfort. Students should not be protected from the challenges of a college education while at college! Moreover, challenging old beliefs and learning new things is often intrinsically emotional. Indeed, if it does *not* connect with an emotion, then it is less likely to be remembered, to really be learned. And sometimes that emotion needs to be encountered, rather than reduced or eliminated by the insulating effect of a trigger warning.

Here, you might invite students to ponder the importance of what sociologists often call "Verstehen," or "understanding by empathy." If you don't put yourself through the process of imagining yourself standing in somebody else's shoes, you deprive yourself of a better understanding of both them and yourself. Ask your students: Even when confronted with opinions or actions we find offensively wrong, doesn't it behoove us to acquire a high-quality analysis of why we find them wrong? Might Verstehen actually be *most* important then?

Walking in a Minefield

Depending on your institution, the topic of trigger warnings can become a labyrinthine nightmare. The Oberlin College faculty handbook, in early 2014, for example, included the following:

> [Experiencing a trigger will] almost always disrupt a student's learning and may make some students feel unsafe in your classroom.
>
> Triggers are not only relevant to sexual misconduct, but also to anything that might cause trauma. . . . Be aware of racism, classism, sexism, heterosexism, cissexism, ableism, and other issues of privilege and oppression. Realize that all forms of violence are traumatic, and that your students have lives before and outside your classroom, experiences you may not expect or understand.[8]

The policy went on to say that "anything could be a trigger" and advised professors to "remove triggering material when it does not contribute directly to the course learning goals."

In the event that a work in the syllabus is "too important to avoid," the policy advised that professors could "hint about what might be triggering about the material," and explain its academic value. For example, it said, "Chinua Achebe's *Things Fall Apart* is a triumph of literature that everyone in the world should read. However, it may trigger readers who have experienced racism, colonialism, religious persecution, violence, suicide, and more." The policy added that faculty members may "strongly consider developing a policy to make triggering material optional or offering students an alternative assignment using different materials." When I was a professor at Tougaloo College, we taught *Things Fall Apart* to freshmen. College students, we assumed, are adults and should be expected to handle adult topics! That being said, here is an important tip: Don't "cold call" on students when discussing difficult or controversial topics such as rape or immigration. There is no need to force students actively and publicly to engage with possibly traumatic subjects. And, of course, deliberately hurtful comments are not to be tolerated in a supportive critiquing community.

But consider the implications of trying not to offend anyone. I once offended an Italian American in Philadelphia by disparaging Christopher Columbus. But if I called Columbus a hero, I'd offend a Native American. So, does it follow that Columbus is not a safe topic? How about God, Jesus, Muhammad, premarital sex, abortion, date rape, the creation of the world, evolution, reactionary Republicans, irresponsible Democrats, vaccines?

This debate about trigger warnings is a problem because it favors feelings over content and the need, sometimes, for productive discomfort. Which is not to say that feelings don't matter. Quite the contrary. Professors do have power, and feelings are always involved in learning. Being a professor is *not* a license to make students feel bad. Professors *should* be diplomatic. Academic freedom is not a license to be a jerk. Moreover, isn't your intention, at least when you are at your best, to help your students learn? Rarely is offending them the best way to accomplish this. So, empathize with students. Treat them the way you would want to be treated when you feel you are in a powerless minority. And embrace the emotional dimensions (and costs) of advanced teaching and learning.

But do not forget that facts and feelings are different things. Unlike factual claims, feelings are not arguable. If a student says, "This class makes me feel afraid," no one can tell her, "No, it doesn't." Thus, if every topic of inquiry must avoid triggering anybody's feelings, every topic of inquiry becomes arbitrarily vulnerable to being buried.

As a college teacher, you need both to serve reality and to facilitate your students' real-world competence. That means you must make and justify some hard choices. Students deserve both emotional accommodation and academic freedom. Denying that these two things can and do sometimes conflict hardly advances your course's mission.

Concluding Thoughts on Beginning the Class

This chapter brings you, the college teacher, some bad news and some good news. The bad news is that, if you hope to transcend the compact of complacency, you've got a fair amount of extra work to do in planning your courses. But the good news is that, when you actually follow through and do this extra work, it pays great dividends for you and for your students. Well-crafted beginnings really are powerful magic. Tossing things together and winging it are, of course, necessary emergency skills for any teacher. (No semesters and very few class meetings ever run to perfection.) But, by purposefully designing our teaching goals, we really can and must do better than "good enough."

3

The Importance of Writing

A colleague at the University of Vermont once said to me, "I'm no longer going to ask my students to write papers. The results are just too deplorable." Because many high school teachers fail to ask students to write papers—perhaps because the results are deplorable—college professors now fail to ask students to write papers, because the results are deplorable. Thus do we progress, from high school avoidance to college-level complicity. Meanwhile, back in the real world, writing prose—even merely a paragraph of instructions for a marketing campaign—is both a required skill for success and a great personal asset. If only for this reason, we must do better.

After thinking and speaking, the third most important social skill is writing well. Your students will be advantaged in life in so many ways if they can write well. It may seem that writing has become less important in the age of instant messaging, but writing even short communications such as emails is still writing.

Gaining the ability to express oneself well in memos, business letters, proposals, personal notes, and so on is a very powerful thing.

This is not just some softheaded personal preference. "Research suggests," the website *Inside Higher Ed* reported in 2015, "that more writing is associated with more learning." The article references the book *Academically Adrift: Limited Learning on College Campuses*, which concludes that college students are not learning enough critical thinking and complex reasoning skills. But it also notes one exception to this trend: "the students who write the most."[1] And make no mistake: No matter your subject, it is utterly crucial, intellectually and educationally, that students write. Writing requires thinking—that is, it requires making the material your own. For both instructors and students, writing means hard work. But writing gets better with practice. You can challenge students not just to write correctly, but to write evocatively, humorously, powerfully. It's our job to teach them, whether in the discipline of sociology, physics, or art. Therefore, never let students say, "I'm not a good writer."

And we should also never bemoan a student's bad writing. No doubt some prior teacher, in college or K–12, told them they were a bad writer or joked about the pain of reading their paper, but neither the student nor we as college teachers can accept that kind of fatalistic laziness. Insist, instead, that the struggling student say, "Until *now* I've not been a good writer." As the late, great Robert Graves said, "There is no such thing as good writing, only good rewriting." First drafts suck. Always. For all of us.

We must get students to realize that writing a good paper is its own reward; that they will have a serious work sample to show people, even their parents! And that they are writing this paper to learn something—something important. Educational psychologist Sarah Rose Cavanagh articulates the two major reasons why well-designed essay assignments are so important. Thinking back to her own college days, Cavanagh recalls:

This [research leading to a term paper] was one of the highlights of my undergraduate career, and the best representation of my idealized portraits of what academia would be when I was an adolescent looking forward to college. . . . [The instructor] had created an assignment for which I had high perceptions of both *control* (I could study almost any topic, in whatever format I wanted) and *value* (I could choose topics that I found inherently valuable and interesting). The result was profound learning. The experience and the content have stayed with me for over fifteen years since.[2]

If you, as the professor, are able to come up with writing assignments that allow for student control, that consider the topics students value, and that require thinking and engagement, students will value those assignments and learn from them. When I taught Race in Film, I required students to write either a fifteen-page report or a five-page report accompanied by a video, a wall project, or other product. Using evidence, including from published writing and/or statistics, students could choose to explore a genre of film, a director, and so on. (Once I received a fine video with accompanying paper about racial images in American musicals.) I even added that if they felt ambitious, they might try to gather data from people before and after they see a movie, to assess its impact.

This was legitimate sociological coursework, and by making sure that students had a say in their research, I aimed to make it worth both their while and my own. Thus, intrinsic motivation works best. Students work because they're interested, because you challenge them, and also because you praise and encourage them and tell them it has to be good because it's important. Emphasizing grades does not bring out the best performance. Emphasizing improvement and good writing does!

So, you must consider yourself a teacher of writing, as well as of sociology (or physics, poetry, the Old Testament, whatever). If you don't teach writing, who will? The student has probably already taken the one semester of writing instruction required by the college. This, however, is never good enough. According to Derek Bok, former president of Harvard University, "Many seniors graduate without being able to write well enough to satisfy their employers. Many cannot reason clearly or perform competently in analyzing complex, nontechnical problems, even though faculties rank critical thinking as the primary goal of a college education."[3]

Still, though, some professors apparently believe that writing is okay for the humanities, but not appropriate for STEM subjects—science, technology, engineering, math. I suggest they have not thought deeply about how writing is like teaching. In the act of teaching a subject (and in the act of writing about it), one realizes what one knows and does not know (even if this realization is not exactly conscious). As one forms an argument and drafts it, revises it, and proofreads it, they do the same. Therefore, just as we professors take our job of teaching our subject seriously and work hard at it, students need to take the work of writing seriously, too.

As we teach our subject, and teach writing, we need to reflect on how best to guide our students in their learning. Simply asking for traditional papers in traditional formats might be a turnoff to many students, and it can also open the door to shoddy or even plagiarized work. By creating assignments that are unique, we also create assignments that invite student ownership and investment. This writing can take various forms: an argument for a policy, a better way to manufacture something, a set of directions, fiction even! Students can do any of these as an assignment in college. The key is that they write clearly. Then, the next step is for them to write evocatively, creating a mood and tone as well as conveying information. Finally, they develop a voice, a style, which will identify the ideas and the words as their own.

I also find it helpful to remember that taking the trouble to emphasize writing and writing skills with students is not entirely about them. Helping your students to write better will undoubtedly help *you* to write better. How could it not? Being conscious of this side benefit can help inspire and sustain your effort to build writing-intensive courses.

Assignments

Many of the hurdles to getting good writing from students can be addressed early on before any writing even occurs. By creating assignments that students find interesting, useful, and relevant, you will end up reading better papers; cutting down on plagiarism, AI-generated work, and cheating; and boosting student learning and engagement with your own subject.

Clearly, some high schools and even some colleges routinely ask students to write formulaic essays that typically require five paragraphs: introduction, three points (each with an example), and a conclusion. It seems this task has become as routine and boring as answering multiple-choice items. Certainly, this task has few counterparts in the real world, after college. So, you should never assign such an essay. Make your essays mirror real-world writing, such as a letter to the editor, a speech that a student will deliver arguing for a position, instructions for completing a task, or something else that someone in your field might actually write.

If you are going to require good writing, tell students ahead of time the basics of what you will expect. For example, I let my students know that I circle errors; when I reach five, I require a rewrite. Tell students you expect a final, clean draft. (Many students have never done two drafts!) Because you have these expectations for the final draft, you also expect them to follow some form of this process: Write the essay. Take it through spell check and grammar check. Print it. Read it aloud. Revise it on paper. Put revisions into the computer. Take it through spell check and grammar check again. Share with another student. Revise to reflect valid feedback. Turn the assignment in.

The first time you assign a paper or project, you may get at least one or two responses that miss the point, at least in some way. For example, students may summarize or (worse) quote various sources at length but fail to make them cohere into an argument of their own. When you point this out, they may reply that they have no standing, that they're not experts, that they thought their *job* was to summarize the thinking of others. The clearer you can be in disabusing students of such misconceptions before they begin, the better results you will obtain. Explain the overall goals you have for the assignment—what knowledge you want students to gain and what skills you want them to master. Tell them the steps you expect them to follow in completing the work, if you have such steps in mind. If you are going to use a grading rubric, share it ahead of time. Again, you will get better results if you do this.[4]

Some teachers require their students to be mind readers, giving only vague instructions for papers. Others are very detailed in what they desire their students to turn in. I fall somewhere in the middle. I think your instructions should cover the following:

1. Approximate length.
2. How to brainstorm for a topic—you can model this in class.
3. How to narrow down their subject. (No sense in reinventing the wheel. I don't want the history of race relations in the United States!)
4. When, why, and how to cite. *When*: when you're including an idea or some information from another source (print, video, interview, etc.). Use quotation marks when you are quoting exactly, and quote exactly when the turn of phrase is important. *Why?* To be honest, to credit those sources, and also to claim their authority. Students can strengthen their argument with a more credible source, so teach them to write a sentence or phrase as to why a particular source is credible and then show them how to incorporate that identification of the source into their text. *How?* Copy the style of any book whose style you accept.
5. How to pick a topic that excites them. Crucial! Encourage them to meet with you as soon as they have it, or, on the other hand, if they cannot seem to find one. The idea is to write a paper that they want to keep five years from now.

Do not disparage better results as somehow a superficial phenomenon because you "spoon-fed" the students with your elaborate instructions. To be sure, it's nice when students don't need help in grasping what you're asking, but you are not really grading them on their ability to figure out what you wanted. Rather, you are asking them to understand and write something substantive about social structure (my course) or poetry or cellular biology or whatever the subject of your course, and that substance is what you want to evoke and then evaluate.

One good way to get across what you want in an assignment is to share a student response that earned an "A" from you in the past. This way, they have an actual model they can look at and refer to. An even better idea: Share an "A" paper and a "C–" paper and ask students, in pairs or small groups, to evaluate them both. Then, you can put the papers online as references, and students can refer to them and to their notes to help them as they construct their writing assignment.

Good writers consider their audience. Students need to understand that their writing makes an impression on readers. And you, their professor, have to expect good writing from them.[5] Tell them you expect them to write well. They need to believe this *in order* to do well.

Students should always spell check and proofread their work, even emails to a professor. One professor I know returns badly written emails and asks for a rewrite before answering. Students are often abashed to reread their poorly written and quickly dashed-off emails. I admit I don't print out my emails to edit them before sending, and people often email from their phones. But in general, I don't think it's a bad idea to print out writing and go over it with a red pen. If email missives are important enough to be revised (and they are!), help your students consider how important revising bigger assignments must be.

In fact, poorly written emails and formative assignments in the first days of class are a good way to find out which students need more guidance and scaffolding. In their article "When a B Isn't Good Enough," Baldasare, Vito, and Del Casino Jr. argue that professors need to catch students who write weakly early in their college careers. Otherwise, the problem may cause bad grades in their junior and senior years and thus lead to them dropping out of school.[6]

I'm also an advocate of encouraging students to make use of legitimate online writing tools. This is an opportunity to reemphasize Robert Graves's vital point that "there is no such thing as good writing, only good rewriting." And the galaxy of useful and honest internet resources—style checkers, not plagiarism databases!—is large. So long as we make clear the difference between polishing and cheating, I think we ought to teach students to avail themselves of this modern kind of help. You might even use some class time to demonstrate how to do so, explaining how you yourself rely on such assets. As well, this is an opportunity to communicate clearly to them what is acceptable and what constitutes dishonest scholarship in your class.

Telling students to think of their peers as their audience is often an excellent way of getting them to think about their readers and their voice. As English professor Rob Jenkins put it in an article in the *Chronicle of Higher Education*, "One of the best things I can do for my students, then, is to provide them with an audience that they just might care about. Clearly, that's not me; they don't care a whit about communicating with me, one human being to another. From me they only care about getting a good grade. . . . Over time, students begin to write for each other—not for me—which leads to better writing."[7]

Another excellent way to help students learn to imagine how their writing will come across is to design what I think of as "real" writing challenges. Through my work on *Lies My Teacher Told Me*, I realized that, for high school students, assigning them to write a three-page introduction to a Native American tribe for next year's students was one great way to make their writing assignments seem like something more than make-work. At the college level, I've encountered many ideas for getting real with my writing requirements. Some of these are:

—Having students annotate a collection in the college archives, so next year's students will know what's in it

—Making additions to Wikipedia entries

—Conducting and writing up a poll, perhaps leading to a student or community newspaper article

—Evaluating research for an organization. (If the course is in nursing or forestry, then evaluate for an organization in that field. If criminology, then for an office that needs your help.)

—Producing a research paper for the class archive as an example to inspire students next year. If it has a community value, then place a copy in the library.

—Remedying a weakness in the textbook or course reading

Scaffolding/Using Resources on Campus

My mentor at Tougaloo College, Ernst Borinski, had a credo: "What a man doesn't know, you must teach him." Some of your students won't know how to write a paper that you want to read. That is where teaching them some writing skills along with the subject matter they are learning in your class will be helpful both for you and for them. Scaffolding your students' learning—doing a fair amount of background, supportive, and preparatory work—will help them draft more readable, more interesting, and better writing. They'll be much more able to exhibit their knowledge to you!

There is no need to do all the work by yourself, though. Engage a librarian to help with your course. Interact with him or her closely; require students to go to the library, and then *require* that each of them make an early "debriefing" visit to your office. By doing so, you may learn some things about what resources are available as you discuss sites, books, and other things that may help your students in their learning process.

Scaffolding needs to begin early in the writing process. And don't be afraid to try using technological tools to help your students. In his article "How a Google Spreadsheet Saved My Literature Class," Erick Sierra, a professor at Trinity Christian College, describes helping his students think about their possible topics, collect their ideas, and receive peer feedback.[8] First, he creates a spreadsheet. Students then edit it to add their viewpoints, questions, and ideas, continuing this brainstorming and virtual sharing process for as long as he thinks is useful. He then edits the document to make space for the students to coalesce their thinking (taking into account each other's ideas and arguments) and to help each of them form strong, personal ideas for their own essays.

Because they can see each other's work, you help them avoid duplicating the arguments of their peers, and, equally, they can find classmates to whom they can direct ideas and questions because they have similar thematic concerns. Also important is that the professor can see the directions the students take and catch them if they go off-track or begin to parrot one another or if their development of an idea leads to an incorrect point, helping to steer them to a better argument. Because they acquire this knowledge in real time, you can confer with students immediately, if the class is small enough. (In addition, since you will have this document, you can also use it to see the development of a student's work, thus discouraging use of AI to generate a final draft.)

I've also used Google slides, assigning a slide to each student to draft introductory paragraphs or other assignments. Because all students are on the same document and are just using different slides within it, it makes it very easy for me to see all their work or to have them read another student's writing and offer feedback. Using spreadsheets, slides, and other relatively simple technological tools to help students write is a terrific way to add scaffolding to your assignments and to help students craft papers that are what you hope to see from them.

While all this work is a great way to get students to engage with their writing, it won't always work. However, because of your efforts, it will make identifying the students who did not follow the process easier. In my Intro to Race Relations class, I created a semester-long assignment to encourage my mostly white and mostly upper-middle- and upper-class students to expand their Verstehen—their understanding of and empathy with others. They were required to attend at least ten hours of events that clearly came from a point of view different from their own race or ethnicity. Then they had to respond to the event in their journal and turn the journal in.

One semester, Ladysmith Black Mambazo, the celebrated all-male South African a cappella singing group, came to Burlington, Vermont. This would be the perfect event for my students to attend, and some did. Two students wrote in their journals about attending the concert and the things they ostensibly saw there. They described the beautiful gowns the women wore, the lovely singing and instrumentation, and how interesting the experience was. Clearly, these two students had not attended. When I called them individually to my office to ask them about their writing, one student quickly admitted that she hadn't attended the concert. The other student was more defensive and recalcitrant. When I asked her, for example, what instruments she saw at the a cappella concert, she replied, "Various." I pressed her to be more specific. "Drums," she answered.

I had tried to make the assignment interesting, unique, and personal, yet still these students had not done the work. But because it was such an intentional assignment, they were not able to use rote responses to bluff their way through the writing, and thus they were accountable for the poor decisions they had made. (I remanded the more combative student to the administration to deal with, as she did not seem fully to understand the error she had made, and I think that's often the right thing to do. One reason to use the institution's procedures is to detect serial cheaters already turned in by other professors.)

Internet Research

As you scaffold these writing assignments, don't assume students know how to do research. Student naivete about search engines is a significant issue. But you can teach them what they don't know! As educational researchers Sam Wineburg and Sarah McGrew report, modern students strongly tend toward "blindly trusting the search engine to put the most reliable results first." While Google's algorithm is far from meaningless, it is also *not* optimized to be a reliable way of sorting truth from fiction—as if such a thing were even possible! In their article "Why Students Can't Google Their Way to the Truth,"

Wineburg and McGrew review the problem and offer several pithy suggestions for how you might help your students recognize and manage their shortcomings in this important area of higher learning.[9]

To demonstrate some strategies for your students, begin to research together with them some relevant topic in class. Open Google and ask students what to do next. Generate their search terms and introduce them to "and," "not," and other Boolean search terms, the importance of quotation marks for restricting searches, the importance of going beyond the first ten hits, and so on.

Ideally, you will be able to spot some unreliable sources and point these out. Websites and articles abound that can help students identify questionable sources, but students don't always know they *should* question sources. "Who gave us the authority to doubt these sources?" they may wonder. You can teach them, though.

Ask them to evaluate the sources, pointing them to Lori Robertson and Eugene Kiely's article, "How to Spot Fake News,"[10] and the Snopes fact-checking website as a start. Try supplying students with two different Wikipedia entries germane to your subject area, one reliable and one not. Help them appreciate the first and critique the second.

Then have them meet with a reference librarian. (Consider taking your entire class to the library, if the class is small enough.) Explain to your class about librarian burnout, caused by vague students with no interests. You don't want to send students over to the library for them to engage in this conversation:

Student: "Hi. I have to write a paper."
Reference librarian: "What about?"
Student: "Um, political science."

Reference librarian: "What course?"

Student: "Urban Politics."

Reference librarian: "Okay, do you have a topic?"

Student: "Um, no, I was hoping you could help me."

Reference librarian: "Well, what interests you in the course?"

Student: "It's not a very interesting course."

This kind of conversation drives reference librarians crazy. Try to create an assignment that is open enough that your students can identify an interesting personal topic that they feel is worth their time and research, but not too broad to cause them to get lost in the possibilities.

Conferencing and Feedback

Your ability to conference with students outside of the classroom will vary depending on the size of your institution, the numbers in your class, and the demands of your semester. You undoubtedly have office hours, and at least some of that time can be spent helping your students understand your assignments and how to complete the work competently. When a student comes to talk to you about a major assignment, you have the power and the responsibility to fashion their trajectory toward a successful outcome. There are several ways to do this.

First, help the student find a topic that is important to her, that excites her, and that makes her want to do the work. This discussion is also a good way to get to know the student and even to influence which subculture of the school she might ultimately be a part of. Perhaps the student sitting before you has never really been pressed to be intellectual about her studies and instead has merely been searching for ways to get good grades. Perhaps she's an athlete and feels like she's just been passed along with whatever work she turns in. If you discover issues that she is actually passionate about, she might find she does the work to further her interest, not merely to fulfill a rubric or to turn something in to her teacher.

Once an appropriate and interesting topic arises, discuss with the student the importance of the topic. If she understands that this is in fact scholarly work and not "homework," she will be impressed with the weight of her own idea and can take further ownership of the assignment. And if the topic is important, it's even clearer to the student that it should be done well, which means you can help her, especially in further discussions, to create a substantive, effective piece of writing.

As students get further into their writing process, require them to print out their title, introductory paragraph, and first source. Doing so will let them know that drafting is an important part of the assignment and that you expect them to put time and thought into it. In class, you can pair students up; one student reads the other student's introduction aloud to the author. This becomes reciprocal and builds relationships within your class. Each student then composes a comment for the author, which allows for immediate and honest feedback from a peer rather than a professor, and an informed peer rather than a friend who isn't in the course and is therefore less familiar with the material or your wishes for the assignment. It also exposes the reader to someone else's writing and helps to illustrate what makes writing effective or not.

(You can, if you wish, assign the students a second partner and repeat the exercise, so that everyone gets two comments.)

Drafts

Require at least two drafts and a one-on-one conference after the first draft. If your course requires a major paper, scaffold the meeting. When you first discuss the paper, require a provisional title, topic, and explanation of the topic, due within a week. That ensures against procrastination. Announce lots of office hours for people who want to talk through their paper topic. Then require an outline of the paper, with sentences rather than mere phrases, and at least two important and useful references, one electronic, one print. Have them share that outline with another class member. It should address why this topic is important to the student. Then, a week before the final draft is due, require a full draft. You should mark up that draft, both regarding its writing and its content. Students will read your comments carefully, because the paper is not a dead letter. Teach your students to look forward to criticism, to editing. It is a gift. To reinforce this credo, include a positive comment on the paper.

Require students to print out their draft, read it aloud to themselves, make corrections, and then have their partner read it aloud to them, even though it is merely a draft, before handing it in to you. Tell students that asking someone to read a draft and find places where they have been unclear is not just okay, but an excellent habit to adopt. If the friend says something is unclear, the idea is to change it until the friend understands. Some part of good writing is having the courage to seek and appreciate such feedback.

Ask students to print out, manually correct, and bring their final draft to a class meeting *before* the paper is due. Devote the first ten minutes of class to peer review. First, generate from class discussion the main points that these papers should make. Next, pair the students up; each student should evaluate the other's paper against those main points and communicate the results to them. Then, have students revise and resubmit at the next class. This gets them using two drafts and seeking feedback from others.

Many students, especially nontraditional college students, are unaware of the importance of accessing helpers in their studies, be they study groups with peers who help them revise and review, professors with office hours, or university writing centers and the many tutors available. A powerful way to let all your students understand that everyone on campus is working hard at learning and relies on other members of the community is to illustrate your own efforts with concrete examples.

Maybe show them a first draft of something that you have now transformed into a polished draft, especially if the first draft was poor, or if your thinking as well as your writing changed a lot. This opens the door for you to encourage really bad first drafts! It's far easier to revise than create. I tell my students that their first draft has a single responsibility: to exist!

Tell students about your own "process." I, for example, always write, then read it on screen and think about it; then revise it; then run it through a basic grammar/style program; then print it out on paper and revise on that copy; then share it with my wife, who offers me advice and critiques; then make changes based on them. Whew! It's always this involved.

Of course, part of the challenge in trying to become a good writer is knowing when and how to stop tinkering and adjusting and get to the final version. Leonardo da Vinci supposedly once said that a work of art is never finished, merely abandoned—meaning that part of the trick of making good art is calling it a day and sending things out into the world. First drafts are (almost) never good enough, but good enough has to arrive at some point, especially in the busy lives of college students and instructors. How do we help our students learn how to get good enough with their writing? What are some of the hallmarks of finished papers?

I would contend the mark of a finished work is that it has "voice."

Once you have students competently writing, you should challenge them to think about their own voice; what makes their writing enjoyable to read? What is personal about their syntax and diction? Do they have a tone they prefer to use? Does it fit the audience? Good writers think about these questions regularly and draft and revise with them in mind. As your students mature as writers, they can be prompted to ask themselves these questions, too.

Some professors give out short rules for students to follow to improve their writing. Linda Elder, the president of the Foundation for Critical Thinking, for example, distills George Orwell's classic writing advice (from his essay "Politics and the English Language") for her Intro to Psychology students:

1. Never use a long word where a short one will do.
2. If it is possible to cut a word out, always cut it out.
3. Never use the passive when you can use the active.
4. Never use a foreign phrase, a scientific word, or a jargon word if you can think of an everyday equivalent.[11]

For me, some of the most important pieces of writing advice include the following:

—Write in a way your younger sibling, or your least academic friend, could understand.

—Write the way you'd speak. Don't use words you wouldn't say out loud.

—Avoid jargon like "problematize," "historicity," "materiality," "hegemony," "paradigmatic." If you must use big words because they are important terms in your field, okay. Otherwise, avoid them.

The educator Sam Wineburg recounts, "I asked third-year Ph.D. students to write an abstract of an article they aspired to publish. In class, I had them put aside their abstracts, take out a sheet of paper, and rewrite the same abstract in language their next-door neighbors or great-aunts could understand. I then arranged students in pairs and had them exchange their laser-printed originals along with their handwritten rewrites." He continues:

> Not surprisingly, students preferred reading the handwritten versions. They were more straightforward, less jargony, and more to the point. But what I didn't anticipate was the heartfelt confessionals that followed. To a one, students testified that rewriting their abstracts in plain language helped them understand at a deeper level what their study was about. In other words, polysyllabic strings of "mediations," "peripheral participations," "hegemonies," and "cultural tools" muddled their thinking.[12]

Students often are so worried about the mechanics of writing that they never think about their audience. This is bad for both the student and their audience. The pioneering composition scholar Donald Murray once observed that many composition mistakes simply disappear when writers care about their audience.[12] So, don't just conceive of your role, vis-à-vis writing, as correcting students' errors. Rather, you are letting them in on how to write well for an audience. That audience might be the general public, fellow students, or people in your field. Their first sentences should grab that audience. Be sure to have a narrative arc and (probably) a chronological organization. Such a structure helps your audience buy into the premise.

Once students feel they've finished their draft, recommend they read their prose aloud. They will hear their own errors. And they'll be able to hear if the writing has good pitch, if it rises and falls, and also if it emphasizes what should be emphasized. Listening to their own writing, they can hear the weakness of "is" and its forms: "Woodrow Wilson's purpose in attacking Russia was to . . ." No! *They've* been studying Wilson and his policies, *they* can speak with some authority! And we should listen to *their* arguments: "Woodrow Wilson attacked Russia in order to . . ."

Another sign of weakness in an argument is the use of passive voice. For some reason, students *love* passive voice. Maybe it's because it helps them get more words in the paper. Maybe they feel it sounds "professorial" (and they might be right about professors relying too much on passive voice). In any case, overreliance on passive voice takes the reader away from the person doing the action, who should generally be the focus of the argument.

Alternatives to Papers

Writing papers is, of course, not always the best plan. Some students will want and need other options. Depending on the size and level of your class, there are plenty of alternatives to papers you can create that will also effectively help your students to improve their thinking and presentation of their ideas.

Poster Presentations

Either as an addition to a paper or as a stand-alone project, have students prepare a fancy graphic illustrating a hypothesis or theme. One big advantage of poster projects is that they open the door to peer interaction and perspective-shifting. You can even do things to intensify these important learning experiences. I think it's a good idea, for example, for students to include a poster when they present rather than each standing up in front of the class and merely talking about their project. That forces students to develop a visual device, as well as to do some writing beyond that for a term paper. Maybe *then* have each student present in front of the class, so all can learn.

You can also gamify poster projects. You might, for example, give every student an envelope on which they put their name and that they affix to the bottom of their poster. Bring a bunch of change to class (for a class of thirty, bring three hundred dimes, three hundred nickels, three hundred pennies; total cost $48). Then, have all the students circulate through the posters, read every one, and "grade" them by depositing a dime, nickel, or penny in the envelopes.

Journals

Some students find it easier to write about their learning when the audience is very small. By definition, a journal is addressed to oneself, with only the instructor getting a glimpse. This kind of writing can be valuable, even uniquely so.

The trick to successful journaling assignments is asking good prompting questions. Some that I like are:

—How will you use this course in your major, your job, your life?

—What do you want me (your teacher) to emphasize that will make the class more useful to you?

—What goals do you have for this course? What do you want to accomplish?

—Why would someone from across the country read your paper?

—Why would someone read it ten years from now? One hundred years from now? What difference does it make?

When we had a speaker coming to class, I incorporated the practice of having the students journal ahead of time various questions they would like to have addressed. I would share those questions with the speaker to help her structure her presentation. Journaling after an online class, a guest speaker, or any video also often leads to good work. A colleague of mine had an excellent practice that I emulated: he would pair students up to ask questions after a guest speaker or movie or performance. Then he would have them journal about the experience of asking their questions and the answers they received.

Electronic Journals

You can achieve a number of beneficial results by having students publish their informal writing online. Online outlets such as blogs or fora serve as a place to try ideas, ask questions, and supply answers. Having students write for an audience other than the professor also forces them to consider their readers, and we've already established how helpful that can be for them as writers. Blogs are very different from journals in that other students will read (and hopefully comment on) the entries. This kind of writing gets students thinking about how their peers might react; they may temper more strident positions, consider their peers' points of view, and be more careful in making their arguments—all characteristics of a good writer!

Ideas for blog entries might include:

—Writing a collective letter to next year's students: how to do well in this course

—Adding to your school's real or hypothetical collection of first-generation college students' mini-biographies (such a thing could be started, if it doesn't already exist)

—Creating possible exam questions

—Sharing useful resources and explaining why they are useful

You might also ask students to create a web page instead of writing a paper. A web page can pack in a lot of elements, including images, lecturettes, maybe music. But you have to insist on quality, including effective writing. And beware: Websites take time, so you need to be able to help students or have a student assistant, campus office, or TA who can.

Book Club Reports

Have five students form a book club in which each reads and reports on a different book related to the course. When I was in grad school, we used to do a similar exercise where we would each write up summaries of essential topics, sociologists, or theories when we were preparing for general exams. By distilling a book's argument down to share with the book club, students are necessarily discerning what is important and what is not so essential, which will help them with their own comprehension and study.

Video Productions

In my Racism in Film course, I had the students supplement their papers with short video clips. You could flip this assignment by making the video the star of the project, with the written portion explaining the need for the video and the context, along with providing explanations of sources and linkages to other course materials.

Final Thought

My overall advice is that you do what it takes to sustain yourself as a passionate advocate and coach of the art of writing. While not the easiest approach, I do think it's the only way to teach college. To embrace its challenges is to do your part to help break the compact of complacency that is steering us toward stagnation and worse.

4

Giving Feedback

You have thought a great deal about the creation of your writing assignments. That intentional work should lead to your students doing a great deal of thinking about their responses to you. Therefore, both you and your students should be invested in the feedback on these assignments! Because of the importance of this feedback, you'll need to be thoughtful, prompt, and purposeful with it. Providing feedback on written work is no less important than any other aspect of teaching college well. If you skimp on or botch this part of the job, you are failing yourself and your students. If you devote sufficient care to it, you can help unlock worlds.

Start the process early. Generally, students need to get feedback from you on their writing before the middle of the semester. That feedback needs to be candid; pull no punches. Require use of the writing center, if necessary, or just offer it as a recommendation, if that's all that is appropriate.

The first time you get a substantial piece of writing from a student, if you have time, have a conference with her about it. You'll want to speak with students who have written badly, including those whose papers show a specific problem that you can address in a short conversation, but consider also including authors of the very best papers, whom you might want to commend in person. (You do want to be sure to give feedback to "A" papers, beyond just the grade.) Invite these already-good writers to go further—to develop a voice, add humor, cadences, and other elements. The advantage of scheduling conferences with the good writers is that students then can't infer that the conferences have a punitive aim.

An early question can be, "What do *you* think of your essay?" Students may be surprised by the query because they didn't really think about their essay at all, in a way. They just "did it." Asking them to reflect implies that they should have asked themselves this question during the drafting period, and they didn't really do much self-assessment. Many students write quickly, don't revise, and hand in the result. In the process, they make mistakes that they themselves would notice if they merely reread their paper aloud. Invite them to do so—just one paragraph, an especially problem-filled one—there in your office. At this point, you can emphasize the simple, expedient way to fix those errors: always print out your paper and read it aloud or, even better, have someone read it to you.

The point is that students need to represent themselves with their best work. Since I teach sociology, I say, "Mary, your sociological ideas don't command my attention because your writing errors communicate that you didn't bother to make a good impression. If you don't take your paper seriously, it's hard for anyone else to." You need to get them to evaluate their own paper before they hand it in. Is it good? Is it great? Very few students will answer yes to the second question.

Occasionally, I have asked students to grade their own essays. You will not apply that grade necessarily, but you might, and you pledge to read and consider it as you grade their work.

Make very sure that when you use peer review, real reviewing is taking place. The biggest problem in peer review is that too many students who should give substantive criticism don't. Remind students about the aim of having your course operate as a supportive critiquing group. Both bravery and kindness are not just indispensable but inseparable in such a group.

If students still don't give good feedback, discuss the problem in class. Ask them what they think of the feedback they "usually get." (That phrasing allows students to say something negative about their reviewer without upsetting anyone because it's in general terms.) Typically, students respond that they don't get enough specific criticisms. Ask reviewers to provide at least two specific suggestions for a rewrite. At least one should be substantive, not grammatical. You might also ask them to talk with each other before reading each other's draft. Tell them not to be shy about stating what feedback they particularly seek. Or have them attach a memo asking their reviewer at least two or three questions about the piece, such as, "Do I need more examples of ____?"[1]

Involving classes in designing their own assessment criteria is another possibility and a way to mitigate mealymouthed student feedback. Having the class develop a rubric helps you communicate to students what is expected in the assignment.

To get students writing with style, you should also have them look at writers with style. In art classes, students often look at other artists' works to learn techniques and styles; why not do this with writing? One great way to jump-start this process: Give them an example of what you consider good writing and ask them to analyze it, discuss it, and then emulate it. Consider having them read Martin Luther King Jr.'s "I Have a Dream" speech:

So even though we face the difficulties of today and tomorrow, I still have a dream. It is a dream deeply rooted in the American dream. I have a dream that one day this nation will rise up and live out the true meaning of its creed: We hold these truths to be self-evident, that all men are created equal.[2]

Note the repetition. Note the allusion. Note the building of clauses. Discuss their effects.

Make sure at the end of the writing project to discuss some of the skills students have (hopefully) learned. This will require you to think about the skills you *want* them to learn. Sometimes this may cause you to alter the assignment, switching the task from "college essay" to, say, an introductory talk to a management group.

John Warner, a college writing professor, has his students write step-by-step instructions for making a peanut butter and jelly sandwich for someone who has never even heard of such a thing. Then he has the students follow their own instructions to a T. Most of the students write quickly, thinking the task is simple and obvious, and neglect to consider their actual audience. When they read verbatim only the words they have written, they realize that they have forgotten their readers! And then they have to make a sandwich with no knife, or with the jelly on the top of the sandwich, or with only a dab of peanut butter, or some other problem that a little more thought in drafting would have solved.[3]

These days, the spread of podcasts and TED Talks has made people more aware of storytelling's power. You might use this awareness as a way of getting students to gain perspective as writers. Historian Richard Marius does it this way: "To write history is to tell a story about the past. Every time we tell a story, we answer questions: On what authority do we tell the story? Is the story true? What parts of it do we know better than others? What caused the events of the story to happen? Are elements of this story like those in other stories we know? What makes this story unique? What makes it worth telling?"[4] Regardless of your subject, students have to be able to identify important moments, link them together in a persuasive and interesting way, and then make the reader understand the value in reading their story.

You might also skim Helen Sword's *Stylish Academic Writing*, especially the first chapter, if you still believe that good academic writing is, well, academic.[5] You might also explore the many associated tools and resources available at Sword's website writersdiet.com. You could even go over a short piece you've published and discuss why you made certain choices and how your process works!

By doing all of this work with them, you let students know that you expect them to pay attention to elements like suspense and propulsion in structuring their own work. I used to ask students to create a title that invites the reader to want to read the article. Then the first sentence should invite the reader to read the second. Why not use alliteration? That's fun and immediately invites the reader into the piece!

Finally, don't ever give in to hostile negative comments. You require a rewrite not for a punitive purpose, but because, as you can say to the student, "your ideas may be good, but I cannot tell for sure, because your writing interferes with your ability to put your best foot forward." It's not your job to rewrite your students' papers; it's your job to assess them and to demand the revisions. Require improvement. In order to let an essay make its full impact, it must be well written. The message you want to communicate is this: "Writing is communication. Writing errors interfere with that communication. It is not fair to the content in this paper for me to grade it in its present form. Also, writing errors make you look incompetent, which causes any reader to look suspiciously upon the content. Finally, many writing errors are so obvious that the reader infers logically that you never bothered to read your paper after you wrote it."

Although I have never tried giving oral comments on papers, doing so seems easy thanks to digital technology. Two Maryland professors, Andrew Cavanaugh and Liyan Song, discuss the positives and negatives of this practice; generally, students like receiving the feedback in audio form and professors save time. Although audio comments tend to be more "global" and less detail-oriented, Cavanaugh and Song found that "students found audio comments clearer than written comments."[6] To my eye, their findings suggest that doing both audio and written commenting is the best practice. Certainly, you want to give your student writers feedback that helps them with both mechanics and analytical skills.

Finally, however you choose to give feedback, do it promptly. If you can't find time to read papers, don't assign them. A key way one's writing develops is via feedback, and comments grow stale quickly.

5

On (Not) Lecturing

With this book, I am arguing that we college teachers must transcend the compact of complacency that prevails in so many higher educational settings. With this chapter, I want to examine how we might do better in our live (including internet-live) appearances in front of our classes. In talking in front of your class, the big temptation is to indulge in some degree of rote instruction. This, of course, is not good enough.

Some professors lecture haplessly. I recall a professor at Tougaloo lecturing to a class of eleven, of whom ten were absent! That is, he was lecturing to one student, until I (his division chair) intervened. (I had him agree to go see each student in the dorm, get them all to come to the next class, and start over.) I also remember a University of Vermont professor lecturing to her Urban Sociology course with five of eleven students present, but not the same five each time, so no continuity was possible. This is education only in a formalist sense, "covering the syllabus," even if few students are along for the ride.

It is also important for those of us who teach college to contemplate the ways in which conventional long-form lecturing is, along with its other problems, itself a discriminatory cultural habit. Education researcher Annie Murphy Paul cites studies showing that "the lecture is not generic or neutral, but a specific cultural form that favors some people while discriminating against others. . . . Students overall perform better in active-learning courses than in traditional lecture courses. However, women, minorities, and low-income and first-generation students benefit more, on average, than white males from more affluent, educated families."[1] This is just one more reason professors need at least some training in pedagogy. Especially at a time when a corps of students are emerging from the grim years of distance learning during the Covid pandemic, professors need to be aware that lecturing might be a disservice to a fair number of their students.

Professors can certainly aid in their students' learning by avoiding lecturing, at least as the predominant style of delivering their course. By employing more active exercises, professors cultivate more engaged students—students who do the reading, do the assignments, and study more. Paul found that this benefit is especially true for demographic groups historically underserved in higher education. For example, for Black students and first-generation college students, the achievement gap was closed considerably by less lecturing. Students who historically are less comfortable in the room—again, often minority students, low-income, or first-generation students—are required to brave the room to ask for clarification of a point. Studies have found that if students do not feel a sense of belonging—as part of a "community of learners"—their academic performance suffers. As Paul writes, "Such obstacles also confront female students enrolled in math and science courses; a 2014 study found that although women made up 60 percent of large introductory biology courses, they accounted for less than 40 percent of those responding to instructors' questions."[2] In classes where the format was reversed, where lectures were delivered outside of class via prerecorded videos and class time was used to solve problems and answer questions, women benefited the most, leveling achievement in the traditionally male-dominated class.

We must keep students from disengaging in class due to any of several factors: boredom, confusion, the environment, or stultifying routine.

Everyone recognizes that lecturing is often a big part of the problem. Think about one of your favorite classes from your undergraduate days. What made it your favorite? Was it the lectures? Taking notes? Certainly not! Many professors know that simply showing up in class and dryly lecturing their students, day after day, is not the best way to excite them. Why then do so many of us still do it?

Well, behind all this willful mediocrity, many silly notions still infest academe, in varying degree, that seem to legitimize rote lecturing. Maybe some of these sound familiar:

—Any other style amounts somehow to spoon-feeding and is a capitulation to students' desires or their shorter attention spans.

—Lecturing is a rite of passage. We had to put up with it; so should "they" (the next generation).

—It's what college is all about, and learning this way is a reasonable requirement for a degree.

—Learning from someone speaking is a necessary skill in life.

Probably some of these ring true to you. I certainly followed some of these when I first started my career as a professor. It seems to me that because most of us were taught that way, that mode of teaching comes to mind first. Some of us never experienced any other style.

But we must do better at choosing, delivering, and, yes, dramatizing our materials.

Non-rote Lecturing

Professors, to be sure, aren't the only ones who cling to stale or convenient assumptions. Many students like lectures because lectures are passive. As Peter Stearns writes in the article "Teaching and Learning in Lectures," students can "park, without thought, or be entertained, or accept authority unconditionally."[3]

However, what college is really all about is not lecturing or being entertained, but learning, especially *learning how to learn*. And we now know that methods other than lecturing help students do that. So, mastering and managing methods other than lecturing are what you need to do to break through the compact of complacency. (In fact, humans have always known this! Where else but the university does long-form lecturing occur? Not in carpentry, not in sports, not—hopefully—in art.) Outside schools, we've always taught through hands-on, experiential learning. Now, that type of learning is not possible in huge classes at college, but that doesn't mean that we have to resort to removing all active learning from our lessons.

Interestingly, in September 2016, the University of Vermont's Larner College of Medicine announced it was abolishing lecturing and has very much followed through! Here is how this excellent, thriving medical school described its progress in 2019:

> The role of the faculty member is changing," says UVM Assistant Dean for Medical Education Katie Huggett, Ph.D., director of the College's Teaching Academy. "They're still sharing their expertise, but in different ways.

Faculty facilitate sessions, rather than lecture. They're becoming content curators, rather than creators.

This shift in how medical students are taught is driven in part by the rapid creation of new medical knowledge, which now outpaces any one person's ability to absorb it. Students need to be able to retrieve information and apply it. In class, they engage higher order thinking skills and learn how to work in teams.

The College's commitment to active learning is based on pedagogical evidence. Research shows that students internalize and retain problem solving skills better when they're interacting with faculty and with peers—the seminal work being a 2014 study published in the Proceedings of the National Academy of Sciences that showed improved grades and exam scores in STEM fields when active learning was employed as compared to traditional lecture.[4]

Luckily, complacent teaching is not only unlikely to succeed; it is also neither necessary nor all that hard to move beyond. What follows isn't an integrated theory of fully transcendent lecturing. It's merely a collection of well-tested ideas and alternatives that I've found to work better, even in large lecture halls, in my decades of teaching at Tougaloo, Harvard, and the University of Vermont.

Preparation

Some classrooms are more conducive to good education than others. To maximize your instruction and the students' learning, make sure you have a strategy for your physical environment from the first day of class. Theater people pay a lot of attention to their sets and settings; you should too.

Block off the back of the classroom, if it is a big lecture hall. Simply stand toward the back and tell students they must sit in front of you. Put someone in charge of enforcing this rule for those who come in late. The first time I ever taught a large class was Urban Sociology, with 113 students at Harvard's summer school. On the first or second day, I asked, "How many of you attend Harvard during the academic year?" Seven hands went up. All seven were seated behind the midpoint of the room and beyond the median student in distance from me.

This was statistically significant. (The null hypothesis: Harvard University students sit randomly throughout the room. In that case, the probability that the first student sits in the back half by chance is 0.5; the probability for the next student is 0.5; the probability that both do is 0.5 times 0.5, or 0.25; the probability that seven do is 0.5 to the 7th power, or .0078. Because .0078 is smaller than .01, statistically, we can reject the null hypothesis as incorrect. That many Harvard students in the back was not due to random chance!) And I had expected this: Harvard students were notorious for "audiencing" their education from the back of the room.

Then I asked, "How many of you attend a liberal arts college with fewer than a thousand students during the academic year?" Maybe twenty hands went up, most seated in the front half of the room, including seven of the ten students in the front row.

I gave a conventional in-class midterm exam. With the help of my TAs, we did a seating chart for the whole room on that day. (A side benefit: Doing so served as a mechanism for flagging possible copying from a neighbor when we graded.) We then graded the midterms blindly and recorded the results in terms of seating location as well as by name. The results: a clear drop-off. The farther back in the room a student habitually sat during the semester, the lower that student's grade on the midterm. There were some A's in the back, of course, and some C–'s in the front, to be sure. But the pattern was clear. Of course, there is the issue of causality: Students who intended to work hard and wanted to participate in class would be much more likely to sit in the front. So I don't claim that sitting in the front in and of itself explains these data.

Ever since, however, in those classes that meet in large lecture halls, I've presented these findings to my students on the first day of class as a cautionary tale. I also make use of various gimmicks to stop "audiencing," including roaming the room, periodically lecturing from the back, and leading exercises in which everyone participates by using electronic handheld transmitters known as clickers. In fact, if I can have flexible seating, then I use a herringbone pattern, with desks angled in a V shape toward the midline of the room so that students face the middle of the class and each other to encourage interaction and engagement.

Once your classroom is established, make your own presence a part of the environment. If there are spaces on the wall, the bulletin board, or in the outside corridor that you can claim for displays or announcements, you can also use these physical spaces to encourage your students to be more active members of the class. Start by posting your syllabus. Get to class early. Talk with students in the corridor. Talk with students while you're putting your outline up on the board. By doing so, you model the engaged behavior you want from the students.

Once you have familiarity with the room, you can now start

preparing the material for the classes to come. To paraphrase Bob Dylan, be sure you know your story well before you start preachin'. Then there's no danger you'll stumble. You might unintentionally leave out a topic, which is why you should carry your outline with you as well as posting it on the board.

As you get your activities and lecturettes (see below) into form, find a mentor, someone who will sit in on your class and give you feedback. Visit their class (and others) to see what tips you can pick up, including what I call negative tips—that is, elements of their class that *do not* seem to work. Ask your TA, if you have one—or a student who dropped in at your office, or a colleague—to help you test the acoustics in your classroom. Ask them to speak with and without the sound system, if there is one, and see if you can hear them from the back of the room. Put some stuff on the board and see if it's readable from the last rows. Decide if there's a point toward the back of the room that you should mark off as forbidden territory, to keep students from vegetating back there. Are there other seats with bad sight lines, bad acoustics, or other distractions?

Always think about why you are teaching something. What big ideas or arguments are you presenting? How does each meeting relate to one or more of these big targets?

And use these big aims shamelessly. As part of the introduction to the class, share the aims with them! I used to think this might be spoon-feeding. Here is one of the silly notions of academe I used to believe: I imagined that students should be able to glean my important ideas from my lecture, and that the effort required to do so was somehow beneficial, that being cryptic like this would somehow lead to more learning. (That's what I'd had to do when I was in college, for goodness' sake!)

However, no evidence supports that line of pedagogy. Listing the important concepts on the board, showing how they will fit together in an outline of the class period, gives students a scaffold that will help them remember not only the major concepts but also details and examples. And it helps them better understand connections and causes, leading to better insight into the big targets of the class and the course. As you begin to plan a class period, consider: What do I want them to know/do by the end of it? Also consider: What do they already know about the topic? This helps to establish what you want to cover in that class period and what your end goals are.

In addition, learn about the sociology of your discipline. Is it overwhelmingly male? Female? White? Do rich people major in your field? Do you want to recruit students to it? Answers to these questions will help inform your teaching.

Keep all this in mind while outlining your lectures. Which, by the way, you absolutely must do! Your posted outline does not need to be masterful, complex, or even very detailed. I came to realize the power of outlining through some painful student feedback. The sociology department at the University of Vermont offered two lecture sections of "Intro Soc" each semester. These were allowed to get large—one hundred to two hundred students. The department talked itself into believing that such huge classes were good educational practice.

Each lecturer was supposed to visit the other's class once during the semester, to watch and perhaps offer feedback. When I did, I noted only 60 students attending, although 120 were enrolled. I too had 120 students, but I averaged 110. I felt smugly superior. I further noticed that the other professor put an outline on the board that had Roman numerals I, II, and III, and each division had an A and a B. Other semesters, I visited on different days, and he again put an outline on the board with I, II, and III, each with A and B. I knew the world couldn't always come divided six ways, and I thought his lectures were predictable, hence boring. Mine were riveting, I thought. That's why I drew greater than 90 percent attendance. I also thought having outlines was "high school." I "thought" (though really, I had not given any thought to the matter) good college students would simply somehow *divine* the organization of my lecture.

Then a student set me straight: "You know why we all come to class? Because your lectures are so disorganized, we can't figure them out from anyone else's notes!"

That remark helped me to see that I had no defensible reason for failing to outline my lectures. Neither do you. The thrill of an "aha" moment can still happen, if you are good and if the material *is* exciting, even though you have in a way telegraphed it via your outline. Your outline need not be boring. It need not be symmetrical. It can even be nearly content free, and it will still work dramatically better than no outline. That is, you can simply put up a "playlist" of what you're going to do.

How do you get started? Invent some twenty-minute (or shorter) modules. Follow them with brief discussions, perhaps in student pairs. That dips your toe in.

For the class I'm about to describe, it might consist of this brief list:

1. Exam review
2. Cognitive dissonance
3. $24 myth

That would be shorthand for this class, in which I:

1. Handed back the take-home exam. From it, I reviewed several items quickly (10 minutes).

Then I noted problems with a four-part item on the essay part of the exam that related to the important concept of cognitive dissonance. After pointing out that cognitive dissonance would be a crucial concept for understanding the rest of the course, I then:

2A. Delivered the first lecturette, on cognitive dissonance (15 minutes).

2B. I asked students to pair up and develop one important (to them) question on cognitive dissonance. I invited the pairs to ask their questions, then answered them myself or threw them to the class for answers (10 minutes). General questions asked of pairs: What are the two main points of the lecturette?

I then asked students to jot down a summary of my main points. That summary would go into their journal. I invited them to compare notes with other students (10 minutes). After that, I:

3. Delivered a short summary of the $24 myth regarding the purchase of Manhattan by the newly arrived Dutch (10 minutes). I ended the class with students answering a question about how they might connect one thing from the first lecturette to something from the second. This entry would serve as the discussion prompt beginning the next class.

That class exemplified seamless transitions between exams, lecturing, listening, participating, journal writing, and (hopefully) discussion among the students themselves after class.

After you put your outline on the board, don't read the outline; your audience already has, since you will give them a few seconds to read it. This frees you to wander the room, engage in eye contact, get into a conversation with part of the audience (in a large class). As you talk with students, emphasize that they must speak loudly, for the folks in the far corners. Watch body language, eye contact. Make sure everyone is engaged.

If your outline is a PowerPoint slide (writing on the blackboard is better—it seems more spontaneous, is always available, and can be referred to repeatedly), turn off your PowerPoint projection, at least until Lecturette #1. (Many lecturettes do not need a PowerPoint, and certainly not as a crutch.) PowerPoints are good in that they appeal to the visual learner, but don't use them as your own prompter, telling you what to say next. You should already *know* what to say next, having practiced your lecturette the night before. However, don't put too much text on a PowerPoint slide! Students write down most of what they see, but doing so keeps them from hearing and remembering most of what they hear. Your overheads *will* get written down. (Your handouts should not be copies of your PowerPoint slides. They serve different purposes.)

For PowerPoint text slides, it's important to remember some basic principles:

—Use 24-point fonts or larger.
—Limit copy to seven words per line and eight lines per slide.
—Make sure you can read your slides from the back of the room.
—When you use maps, choose versions that will xerox well in black and white.

As you plan your class, think about what students will make of this new information. Is it necessary? Is it interesting?! Is it comprehensible? Make sure to avoid jargon. If you cannot say what you want to say in clear, understandable language, maybe you do not understand it yourself. Of course, I recognize that you must introduce students to special terms in your discipline, from "hadron" to "iambic" to "Verstehen." But those must be the exceptions, not the rule. Practice out loud, preferably to a friend or companion not in your field. Does she understand what she hears? Does she find it gripping? Clearly mark in your notes where you should be halfway through your presentation time, when you have ten minutes left, and five minutes left. Put brackets around optional stuff you can cut.

Usually, it's best to begin your lecture with a "hook." For example: "What does [your topic] have to do with *you* in particular?"

Another good hook is a rhetorical question. These set up a tiny storyline and can create a moment of suspense: A pause throws the question to students, gets them thinking, even if you don't then call on them. Your audience then takes the answer as a mild "aha!" because it clears up this momentary mystery. Rhetorical questions or even actual questions draw students in, making it more of a conversation and getting students caring about what you're presenting. You can also impose a narrative arc onto a topic. In a class on gentrification, for example, I'll ask: "Where do we want rich people to live?"? Do we want them to all live in one place?"

Or, you can ask students several questions at the beginning of the hour. These can be printed on a handout or appear on a PowerPoint slide. They can be matters of fact, such as the percentage of African Americans in the U.S. population or why the South seceded, or matters of interpretation, such as which person is right in the debate about the effects of segregation in the United States, Gunnar Myrdal or Francis Cecil Sumner. Then, during the hour, you can return to the questions as appropriate. See if answers have changed at the end of the lecture. Feel free to let the question sit. Wait. Silence is okay. By waiting, you allow students to understand that you want them to think about these things.

To both better understand the class's general comprehension and teach important aspects of your field, another possible "hook" is to introduce students to their own misunderstandings in a novel way. This allows you to see where their misconceptions are and will help them feel the impact of a surprising reversal of a long-held understanding, a sort of "Eureka!" moment where something becomes clear to them. In sociology, one exercise I find very meaningful and edifying particularly because it reveals basic tenets of the field is to ask students to fill in a simple six-cell (two rows of three) chart based on the following prompt:

> In January 1971, George Gallup polled Americans about their feelings regarding the war in Vietnam. The poll stated: "A proposal has been made in Congress to require the U.S. government to bring home all U.S. troops before the end of this year." It then asked: "Would you like to have your congressman vote for or against this proposal?"
>
> In the space below, which has been constructed in standard format for tables in sociology, fill in your best guesses as to how the response went, by educational group. Note that the overall response in January 1971 was 73% in favor of withdrawal. But, of course, this percentage might vary by educational grouping. "Don't knows" are excluded.

Assume that your table is correct. Develop at least two
reasonable hypotheses or causal arguments to explain it.
(In other words, assume that the data really did come out
as you guessed they would. Why?)

Students then fill in percentages for all six boxes, identifying which
of the following groups were more hawkish about continuing the war
and which were more dovish: college-educated respondents, high
school–educated respondents, and respondents with less than a high
school education. By the end of the exercise, the students and I have
arrived at a discussion about why they incorrectly assumed (which is
almost always the case) that more educated people were more dovish,
and what that assumption says about how our society is structured. It
is an excellent introduction to methods, terms, and ideas in the field.
Your field undoubtedly has analogous exercises!

Showing students the importance of "mere" facts can also serve
as a lecture hook. A big problem in lecturing is the lack of student
knowledge on which to build. While every generation has doubtless
derided the ignorance of the next, the web and social media have perhaps made the situation worse for today's college students, who feel
they can simply ask Siri or Alexa anything they don't know. There
is also the simple issue of the age of most college students: In 2024,
the typical first-year college student was two years old when Barack
Obama won the presidency. Is it reasonable to expect them to recall
anything from when they were two? Do you recall anything from
the presidential campaign when you were two? About current events,
students are not much better informed. Professor John Haas noted in
2017 that many students had no familiarity with "the Taliban," with
whom the United States had been at war in Afghanistan since 2001.

Then there are plain deficiencies in vocabulary: terms like "affluent" and "terra incognita" are often unknown territory.[5]

We cannot simply bemoan these problems; we must reach students where they are. One way to deal with students' limited vocabularies is by providing helpful contextual clues when using unfamiliar words, as I just did with "terra incognita." Another: Ask students at the beginning of the year to wave a hand whenever they don't know a word. Reward hand-wavers by commending them, then asking, "Anyone else not familiar with the term?" If no one else waves, call on any student and ask for the meaning. If her definition isn't adequate, ask, "Who can help her out?" Make sure students understand you seek to know what the word means—in plain English, not an elegant definition. In general, rewarding students for asking questions will help you to be a better teacher as you come to see where their gaps in knowledge are.

One thing to consider as you contemplate this situation is whether the best way to introduce new facts and material is always for students to hear about it from you. Maybe they should *read* the material first, perhaps with assigned questions in mind, and then discuss it as their next encounter with it. Or maybe a video should be their first encounter with it, followed by a discussion.

Lecturettes

I do propose that you lecture—just not for every minute of a fifty- or seventy-five-minute class period. I suggest lecturettes—ten minutes long, twenty at the most, with a beginning and an end. You want to punctuate the remainder of the class time by eliciting student participation through various means.

When you choose to lecture, first and foremost you need to be passionate about what you are presenting. It needs to have affected you personally. If it does not, why are you telling others about it? Leave it out! If you teach literature, teach what you love. If you *have* to include a poem by Emily Dickinson, whose work perhaps you don't like in general, find at least one poem of hers that you do like. Or, teach *against* Dickinson, but announce ahead of time that you will do so, first asking your students who among them *likes* her poems, and having them meet with you and prepare a talk within your talk, giving a positive view of Dickinson or at least of one her poems. Or invite a guest colleague.

Have some presence. If you are quiet and retiring, choose to be different in lecture. You want students to know that you have something important to convey to them that day. Rather than, "Okay, today we have to cover a lot of stuff, so let's get going," try instead, "Today we have a crucial concept to understand: [fill in the blank]." You always want to convey that you feel what you are teaching is important.

Look good. Just as an actor takes care with their makeup and clothing, you should make an impression from the start. Curate your own look. I generally don't wear a tie, and I take off my sports coat if it's hot. I tend to be folksy and less formal, and hopefully thus less aloof.

Before class, consider jotting one or two questions on the board for the students to respond to in their journals (their responses can be in electronic form). For the very first class of the semester, the question "How does the topic of this class relate to your intended career?" can generate remarkably personal stories. Students will write a lot if they know that you will reply, so reply promptly.

For later classes, you might choose a question that you also posted in your course outline for the day or at the start of that unit. You might begin class by having students write a five-minute essay to answer a question that is basic but can elicit great responses. That will make sure discussion won't fall flat. Or use the "think/pair/share" discussion strategy: Ask the students to think about a question silently for a minute. Then, pair them up and have them share their thoughts with a partner, which will help them further develop their understanding and refine their articulation of their idea. Finally, have a short class discussion where people can share their idea, comment on a partner's, or introduce questions or difficulties that arose. Now, the whole class is involved and has already added to their understanding of your topic of choice.

However you begin a lecture, don't neglect to post the outline and to refer to it. And whichever kind of outline you use, begin class by summarizing its main points. Employ the old public-speaking adage: State what you're going to do, do it, then reiterate what you did. As you go through the topic's main points, be sure to speak openly about its implications—why it's important. You will come back to this at the end, no doubt, but students need a reason to "buy in" to the topic from the start.

And here's the twist: Don't overprepare.

Let the course breathe. Remember, your job isn't just presenting content. You need to find out what your students are *doing* with the content. Are they learning it? Can they talk about it, rather than merely regurgitate it? Has it meshed, contradicted, or otherwise made a difference with respect to what they think in other spheres, or what they thought before they took your course? The only way to find out these things is by having *them* speak.

Remember that asking students what they already know about the pending subject is often a good way to start any class. This gets them thinking about the matter at hand. It can also provide you with important information about what students know and don't know, information that may change how you teach that day. Try giving students a minute or so to write down what they know first. This prework helps ensure that every student has something to say. Writing in the first minute of class also signals the class that something important is happening, so it's time to be in class mentally as well as physically. Of course, beginning with something important makes it more likely that students will arrive on time.

During class, refer to your outline on the blackboard from time to time; show where you are on it. Announce, "This is important!" Use repetition and signal why you are doing that: "So you can get it down in your notes." That implies students are taking notes, which is good. Indeed, *tell* students to take notes. Some don't know! Tell them what is important, too, although not so often that they can infer that when you *don't* say it, they need not take notes.

Early in the semester, stop five minutes before the end of class to ask students to underline and organize their notes. Then ask them to draft a three-minute "speed write" of what was important that day. Alternatively, begin the *next* class by asking for a three-minute "speed write" of what was important the day before. That's a good way to get students settled in to learn. Sometimes I have asked students to do this without recourse to their class notes or their journals. That helps ensure that the material actually made it into the cerebral cortex, not just onto the page or into the computer file.

After finishing an item on your outline, go over to it on the board, draw a slash through part of it, and say, "Moving on now to . . . [the next item]." You will be stunned at how much this improves your teaching evaluations, because your students will look back feeling that they knew where the presentations were going, how they unfolded, how they ended, and how we got there. Also, as a resource for students, put your lecture and notes online. It can be time-consuming, but record your own lectures. Watch them and look for opportunities for improvement. Condense them to eliminate dead air and mistakes, and post *those versions* online for next year. Then use next year's class to discuss the lectures. This is akin to "flipping" the course so the lecture takes place outside the classroom and so class time is used instead for active discussion and student engagement. Some students do not learn well from lectures or need to hear them a second time; help them out by providing alternatives.

When you get a tough question in class, model someone who considers other points of view. Make sure you don't "listen to rebut." If the question is halfway useful or can be made to be useful, you want to begin your reply with, "What a fine question!" That also gives you a moment to gather your thoughts. Then, think out loud, in front of the class. That helps your students see and hear how you think, rather than just presenting them with an answer.

Your outline for the day is a guide, not a straitjacket. A really good student question or comment may take you on a trip different from the road map you had put on the board. A really bad question or comment may convince you that something basic has been misunderstood, so you must use this teachable moment to correct the problem. Or you may simply get in "a zone" of your own making, going off on a tangent that in the moment seems important. Fine—but save time at the end to go over to the board and explain what you covered and did not cover in your outline, how the things you discussed relate to the matters at hand, and what, if anything, you will do to cover the rest of the items on the board. Don't let your outline hang there on the board, orphaned, dying under the lights.

One way to communicate your passion for your subject is your energy! If you remain motionless droning on from notes, your students will take your unintended cue. So, don't just stand behind the lectern. At the least, come out to the front for some important point, or when you switch to discussion mode. Have another teacher watch you practice teaching in the room (and take a video). Maybe you'll learn to stop walking around so much. Maybe you'll want to move more and not be trapped behind a podium. Maybe shorten your sentences; maybe organize your paragraphs. Do you drop your voice at the tail end of sentences? Do you speak too quickly? Do you have long rambling sentences? (I did. I watched a video of myself teaching and realized that I fell into discursive speaking even though I wanted to be focused and to the point. It certainly changed my process of lecturing!) Do you ever use your hands? Try it, once in a while—maybe a clenched fist held upright as you say something crucially important.

Use the whole room. Some time, early in the class period, go up to the back row and lecture for a minute or two from there, engaging the students who are in the back. Also, go up the aisle a bit and look at a particular section as you ask a question, especially if that section has been quiet.

Move mentally, too. Remember to travel back and forth between details and wider insights. Hypothetical questions and scenarios can help. For example, ask students to imagine that they are an intern at Khan Academy. They have a mass of data showing that Black and Latino people who are asked to specify their race at the start of an exam do worse on that exam than Black and Latino people who are not asked about their race. How would your students represent that finding visually to convince people? Ask them to locate and write up research and theory to lend context to that finding. Now they will go off and perhaps on their own learn about Claude Steele's research on stereotypes in his book *Whistling Vivaldi*, as well as want to learn about bar graphs, histograms, and so on.

Never just read your lecturettes to the students. *Deliver* these set pieces as talks. You can read aloud when you are quoting someone else—an authority in your field, a poem, a nonfiction paragraph you want to discuss as an example of good writing or bad writing, an original source. (For example, I have read a Walt Whitman poem that introduced the topic of "socialization," or a racist diatribe from the resident of a sundown town defending its exclusion of African Americans, or an evocative description of social status from Thorstein Veblen's *Theory of the Leisure Class*.) Such readings make for a different experience than that of a lecture, so it provides variety for the class. Clever use of primary sources can also enliven the classroom experience. I have sometimes asked students to study William Jennings Bryan's famous "Cross of Gold" speech. But instead of just talking about the speech, I have had a student stand up and declaim it. It works! In fact, you might ask each student to declaim a classic or crucial reading segment once a semester.

You can use notes, of course, when you lecture, but know what you will say regarding each note. Illustrate every generalization with an example, if appropriate. The example—the anecdote—makes it come alive and helps students remember it. In a sense, your twenty-minute lecturette can be built out of a series of thirty-second segments, each prompted by a note on your (single) piece of paper.

If you have done all these things—if you are being conscious about what you are teaching and why you are teaching it, and you have been purposeful in your organization and delivery—you should have an engaged and thoughtful audience. Be aware of what you did to get it there.

And once the audience is there, you can take some chances! If you are about to go out on a limb, announce it. "Most professors of [your discipline] think _____. They may be right. However, *I* think _____." The tentative nature of your announcement ("They may be right") can lead to a good short discussion. "What do *you* think?" This gambit places your students in the position of arbiters of the field, it serves as a compliment to them, taking their conclusions seriously.

Just as ability and even intelligence can be learned, so can what Erving Goffman termed "impression management" which is the attempt to influence people's perceptions in a social interaction; even physical or (more accurately) visual impression management can be learned. And once you learn it, you will become a better teacher.

Alternatives to Lecturing

Variety is the spice of education. Some people respond well to the spoken word. Others do better reading: Perhaps they can read faster than most people speak, or they benefit from being able to go back and reread a passage. Still others learn best in small groups, where they can talk, try to teach and learn from others, and ask questions. Moreover, after they leave school, your students will be exposed to and will need to operate in different instructional approaches, so they may as well get accustomed to them now. Finally, using different approaches is less boring—even for you—than simply talking all the time. So, teach in diverse ways, especially in large lecture halls. Never just talk for more than twenty minutes without some change of pace—a probing discussion question, a movie clip, something!

Don't lecture at all about topics others have lectured on better. Star lecturers have put up online courses on the great philosophers, introductory economics, modern American literature, astronomy, and almost everything else. Often these lectures are highly produced, with useful video clips, maps, visits to the places discussed, and so on. Use them! Show a fragment, then stop to ask questions or to make it relevant to the day's headline or to your student population. As mentioned earlier, you may also want to "flip" part of your course—that is, ask students to watch on their own computers, on their own time, individually or in groups, then use class time for questions, discussions, and other activities better done in person.[6]

Posing actual questions is also good; they involve the class, even if the same few people do most of the responding. And, of course, the professor can always pair up students to answer, then call on the pair. A simple question for the class might be: "What are three main points of my lecture thus far?"

You know you want your students engaged and involved. Therefore, do not allow laptops or phones to be used during your class! Students should first take notes on paper. Then they may enter them into their computer.[7] Studies show that students learn more from taking notes by hand on paper rather than by typing on a laptop or tablet.[8] Taking notes by hand is slower than typing and thus requires in-the-moment editing, synthesizing, and paraphrasing the most relevant points, all of which require heightened processing and comprehension on the part of the notetaker. I would argue that even most of those students with an accommodation for in-class use of a computer could benefit from taking notes by hand.

Because you will almost certainly get pushback on this policy, you ought to point out that not only is the question eminently research-able, but serious research has already been done. A study in the *Journal of the Association for Consumer Research* found that student subjects who kept their smartphones on their desks (facedown and on silent), "rather than in a backpack or stashed in another room, performed worse on tests of attention and cognitive processing. The difference was biggest among students who reported being the most attached to their smartphones."[9] In *The Distracted Mind*, researchers Adam Gazzaley and Larry D. Rosen point to three separate studies that found "when people engaged in a conversation with a cellphone present but not in use . . . they tended to rate the quality of the conversation lower, or rate their relationship with their conversation partner lower, than when those conversations were conducted without the presence of cellphones. The mere presence of a visible device . . . led people to focus less on the person in front of them."[10]

Sometimes, entire university departments summon the courage to act on the accumulating evidence that new media devices hinder classroom learning. In 2016, the Communications Department at California State University at Dominguez Hills banned smartphones, laptops, and other electronic devices in every class. The school argued that "true multitasking is a myth. Our brains focus on one thing by shutting out other things. We can't pay attention to two things simultaneously, such as reading a text string while listening to a teacher's instructions."[11]

What Students Should Do During Lectures

You may discover that some students write down everything in class. Other don't take notes; they just sit and listen. Neither is an effective way to learn. Both approaches are similar, respectively, to the reading approaches of highlighting everything and taking no notes at all. Teach students why and how to take notes on a lecture.

You can do things to help students learn good note-taking habits. When you are speaking, tell them when to take something down. Don't consider this spoon-feeding. Frequently give them a spoiler alert that the next point is important and should go into their notes. As you do this throughout the semester, they should start noticing when and how you deliver important points.

As students become more adept and consistent in their note-taking, make use of students' notes. For example, call on a student to ask what she wrote for the definition of an important term that you defined in the previous class. If she only wrote what you said, ask her to repeat it in her own words, or give an example. You might announce a quiz for the next class and say, "You can use your notes for this quiz." Then ask, after the quiz, "How did that change your note-taking?"

Invite them to compare notes with other students. Pairing up helps students see what they may have missed. Taking notes is important to the group as well. It communicates to the professor and to other students that you take the course seriously and are learning something.

Wrapping Things Up

Finally, don't waste the chance for a good conclusion to each class meeting. At the end of class, always allow at least a few minutes to ask: "Did we achieve the objective with which I started the class?" See what they say! Or ask, "Did we cover everything in the outline?" If not, what should you do? Maybe solicit questions for next time. Or ask: "What was the most important point of today's class?" Or, "What question is uppermost in your mind from today's class?" The answers to these questions can form the basis of your introductory hook for the next class.

Near the end of class, you might have students write a one-minute summary of what was covered in it. Many teachers call these "exit tickets." Discuss immediately. Such an exercise will not only help your students coalesce their understanding but also help you identify information that needs reviewing or reteaching in the near future. Their responses to these prompts will shine a guiding light into your next class.

6

Readings

Thoughtlessness can plague the raw material of every college course: the assigned readings. Reading is, despite the times, the inescapable foundation of good college teaching and learning. Yet it remains tempting to think otherwise. Some people say nowadays that students cannot be expected to read actual books. "They don't have time," or "Now they're used to reading tweets and thus books are too long and too hard," or "The web has undermined literacy!"

When you come across this common excuse in discussions with your students or colleagues, you might want to point out that, among other things, it's not new. Fifty years ago, the same charges now levied against the new media were levied against television. Yet people still read books today. And it turns out that the same charge was once upon a time levied against books themselves—that they distracted students from learning and thinking! This, though, isn't a reason to surrender. On the contrary, I endorse sociologist Frank Furedi's conclusion: "Literacy comes into its own when people read what matters to them. Instead of blaming our supposed Age of Distraction for turning the lecture hall into a digital playpen, we should think harder about how we can earn the attention of our students."[1] You have to make it in students' interest to do the reading, and you have to let them know what you expect of them.

Books—print books—matter a very great deal. Students themselves know this to be true, even if they wish it weren't. According to an article in the *Chronicle of Higher Education*, when linguist Naomi S. Baron, the author of several invaluable books about reading, asked over four hundred college students in five countries "[in] which medium they concentrated best when reading," 92 percent answered print.[2] If readers interface only with screens they are conditioned to skim and scan, Baron argues. It is difficult for students to read deeply when they scroll through Baldwin or Chaucer in the same way they consume headlines from CNN.

In your course outline, you may want to tell your students how to read. "What?" you may think! "I can't teach reading! And besides, my students already know how to read." Still, some of them—and not just first-year students—may need to learn how to read and master large amounts of material, take notes, and study for a course (or for other purposes later).

It's important that students do the reading *before* the lecture or discussion section for which the reading is assigned. They should annotate the reading by both highlighting and making notes in the margins or on separate paper. Then they should have those notes and the reading out in class for reference to be certain that they've identified the most important aspects and have clarity about the concepts of the reading.

A key to good reading is to put the material into your own words. So, ask students not just to highlight or underline, but to write brief chapter summaries at the end of each chapter. Then call on a student to put their summary on the board to start discussion.

Show students how to highlight. Ask them each to highlight an article, then pair them up and have them compare results. They shouldn't highlight too much! First-generation college students may not know that highlighting 80 percent of a text does not work. Conclude by showing *your* own highlighting.

And once you have taught those note-taking skills, think about how you can reinforce them in your lessons. Allow for open notes on some assignments. Ask students to reference their notes in a writing assignment or in discussion. Have small groups pool their best annotations and turn them into a presentation, a slide show, or a video.

Because you have considered the readings and decided they are necessary and useful, you are also invested in having the students actually read them. If you find that students have shown (via test answer or sluggish discussion) that they may not understand a key concept or issue or reading, you need to check in with those students to help them with the material.

What to Assign

If the basic aim of your course isn't to convey as much technical knowledge as possible into your students' minds, then you may want to reconsider assigning a textbook. If you are assigning one, why? Have you really thought this decision through? Does it help you get across those things that you consider truly important? Does it help you teach students how to read and think and write in your discipline? Or is the textbook mainly a repository of content—important content, to be sure, but mostly preliminary to what you really want to convey?

Sometimes professors adopt textbooks because they provide a shortcut: they organize your course for you, and include the imprimatur of someone else, someone important. If the textbook's prose puts your students to sleep, however, or if it emphasizes facts over process, "knowledge" over skill, then adopting a textbook makes your course worse, not better.

All too often, the textbook is the only reading or the main reading in a course. Even when it is flanked by half a dozen ancillary readings, the others can assume a position of lesser importance in students' minds, if not in your own. Some readings should be in tension with each other. Consider, for example, the debate between E. Franklin Frazier and Melville Herskovits on slavery's cultural impact on enslaved people, or that between Margaret Mitchell and Margaret Walker on the basic story of American racial slavery. There are similar canonical yet opposing views in virtually every subject area. Which view is correct? How do you settle on one or the other?

Good textbooks do play important functions, in both general and inherently technical, scientific, or mathematical courses. In introductory courses, they organize the field, providing a sort of road map to its important elements. Some students may find themselves referring to their introductory textbook years later, as they prepare for their senior seminar, or later still, as they prepare for gatekeeping exams in graduate school. If you do *not* assign a textbook, instead using only a batch of (probably catchier) readings, it will fall to you to hold these disparate elements together in class.[3]

The decision on whether to use a textbook need not be an either/or one. You can use a textbook for part of your course. You can use part of a textbook in your course. You may even use one chapter of a textbook as a *bad* example, asking students to expose its errors and omissions. Then you are using the book creatively, as a tool rather than a crutch. Do be mindful of student finances, however. Students may legitimately complain if they have to pay big bucks for a hardbound textbook, only to find that you make use of only a couple of chapters.

For non-textbooks: Above all, assign books worth keeping. Then suggest that students should keep them. At least one. And don't be afraid to lightly shame students if they have sparse book collections. In my teaching career, I often told my students about my informal project I undertook as a undergraduate during a "semester abroad," when I spent time at both Tougaloo and Mississippi State University, of observing how many books students in both places had in their dorms and apartments. Since MSU is the larger, better-funded school with the bigger and more privileged student body, most people assume that the MSU students back then must've kept more books at hand. Quite the opposite, though, was my clear finding. At MSU, the twenty-three students on my floor owned fifty-one books among all of them (one person accounted for forty-two of these.) Most of my dormmates had no books in their rooms! By contrast, at Tougaloo, my four roommates alone owned forty-eight books among them, about a dozen each. Books and power have always been closely intertwined, and it can be inspiring and enlightening to talk directly about this.

Another reason to assign books is that book culture tends to be self-reinforcing. The passion pays its own dividends. According to an article by sociologist M.D.R. Evans and colleagues in the journal *Research in Social Stratification and Mobility*, documenting research on books and schooling across nations, "Children growing up in homes with many books get 3 years more schooling than children from bookless homes, independent of their parents' education, occupation, and class."[4]

Having one book might lead to having another. A student who has books in their dorm room is reminded that owning them is a good idea. It defines it as a place where an intellectual subculture exists and defines one as a member of that subculture.

Since you have been thoughtful and careful in choosing your readings, including respecting student budgets, you should encourage your students to buy the books you assign—unless they are available from the library, online, or in other ways—and to read them. On the first day of class, explain why owning the readings is best.

Once you establish a culture of students reading and discussing the material—essentially becoming intellectuals!—you need to remember that good teaching requires reinforcement and practice to make a skill reliable and effective. So you have to scaffold your reading assignments to make sure that students understand them and can find the relevant takeaways in the texts. Perhaps you make sure they have a list of the difficult vocabulary in the text, or you break the reading into smaller chunks along with some guiding questions. You might even include a brief summary of the text for students to use as a primer before they read the text.

In using books, the sailing doesn't always have to be smooth, either. In some cases, bumpiness can be your friend. Learning from your students about the bumpy parts can be a teachable moment for them as well as for you. Sometimes, for example, it's not obvious that a reading selection is hard, even when it *is* hard. In sociology, a famous reading (and common reading assignment) has been "The Promise," the first chapter of *The Sociological Imagination*, the 1959 book by C. Wright Mills. Professors have assigned it to undergraduates for decades. It is very widely supposed to be an evocative introduction to the field. Many sociologists remember fondly the impact it made on them and think it will have the same transformative effect on their students.

I assigned it to my first-year students at Tougaloo, only to learn that many students found it opaque. I learned this when I quizzed students closely about it in my office. They had done the reading—Tougaloo was a demanding school—but parts of it had gone past them without leaving any residue of understanding. Eventually, I reread it myself and realized that it was neither as transparent nor as enticing as I had remembered.

While writing *Lies My Teacher Told Me*, I read eighteen high school textbooks of U.S. history. (I'm possibly the only American ever to attempt this feat.) That experience convinced me that professors should never assign a textbook without reading it. Indeed, you should never assign a *chapter* without reading it first. Too often, books that *look* interesting prove deadly dull when actually *read*. Also, as some publishers cut back on overhead, editing and copyediting disappear, leading to careless writing errors that can make an entire paragraph incomprehensible. *You* need to discover the problems. It's embarrassing when students discover them. Moreover, students may *not* discover them, or at least never bring them up, thinking themselves, rather than the text, to be at fault.

And take heart, because the judicious, intentional use of imperfect or challenging readings can often lead to valuable teaching and learning opportunities. Are important ideas always easy to locate in a text? How might *we* improve on stunted or stumbling versions of classic arguments? Why hasn't somebody already done so? These are fruitful questions you can raise, provided you are up-front about your assignment choices and out in front of your own reading agenda.

How to Reference Readings in Class

Now that you've thought about what your students should be reading, and now that you've helped scaffold the reading task for them, you need to think about the role the reading will play in class. The first moment to do this is when you are assigning the reading. When you introduce the next reading, explain why you chose it. What is it supposed to do for your course? Why are you assigning it *now*? Give students a sense of what the reading is going to be about, what challenges they may face in reading it, and what ideas are crucial to better understanding it.

However, don't supply a "pony"—a literal translation—so they only have to skim it. Rather, aim them toward the key passages. Just as an outline helps students to follow a lecture, introducing the reading will help your students understand where the class is going, aspects of the reading they might be on the lookout for, and ways they can create connections between the course and the assignment.

If you assigned the reading, it must have something in it you want to make sure they have comprehended! One way to ensure that that happens and to address anything that needs clarification is to ask students to submit a one-sentence summary of the reading's "main idea," via email, at least an hour before class. Or have them choose one sentence from the reading, again via email, that they want to discuss—a sentence that moved them, confused them, that they thought was most important, whatever. Refer to some of these emails, especially if they are good, or if they are offbeat but defensible and useful. Or you could have the students discuss their sentences in pairs; after one minute on each sentence, ask the pairs to bring one of their sentences before the whole class if they feel it's a good choice.

Include credit for these responses in your grading. Or have students post their answers for the class, via class email, the Blackboard course management system, or whatever technology you use. You can then ask students to submit to you their three best posts at the end of the semester.[5] You should grade only those, but make sure they posted the required number of times. Make sure to use posts in class. Maybe show a really good post and discuss why it's good. Or pick one that asks a good question and use it to prompt a ten-minute discussion in class.

How to Engage Students with Readings

As instructors, we know that teaching something once and expecting it to be mastered is not competent instruction. A person needs to practice a skill both with assistance and on their own to become comfortable and flexible enough for the skill to be useful and effective. So it is with readings. Don't have students merely do the reading and think that's sufficient. Make sure that they have to engage with the information, using it in discussion, in writing, in rebuttals, and that they repeatedly do so. There are many ways to accomplish this.

One of my favorite activities is a "concentric circles" discussion group. This can certainly be used to discuss the reading from the homework—and any topic, for that matter. Students sit in two circles, a small one facing outward and a larger one facing in. A question or comment is then raised about the reading, and each student discusses it with the person seated across from them. After a set amount of time, one circle rotates, each student in it moving down one chair so that they are now facing a new person, and the conversation can proceed or a new question can be introduced.

This technique allows for a number of excellent conditions: people are paired with those they might not normally be paired with; it can produce a mix of factual and deep questions, either raised by the professor or arising naturally during discussion; it automatically involves everyone in the class without the pressure of a large audience; and it avoids the monotony and other drawbacks of a lecture, priming the students for a return to a whole-group discussion or even a lecturette by you, which they will now be ready to interrupt with relevant comments and questions!

Here is a final recommendation for ensuring full engagement on assigned reading: "Jigsawing"—dividing reading into sections and assigning them to different readers—is an effective method of both teaching a topic and making sure that students are engaged with and responsible for the material. I happened upon it when a class told me that they wanted to read my dissertation, which covers the upward mobility of Chinese immigrants in Mississippi. By assigning certain parts of the material only to certain students, who were then responsible for teaching their part to the rest, the assignment got students to read just a part of a large work and become class experts on it. Because only a few read that chapter and they are responsible for teaching it to the other students, it galvanizes discussion, with students asking each other questions, because they want to know all about the story—how it began, developed, and ended. The technique saves time and teaches cooperative learning, which will be helpful later in graduate school and with problem-solving on the job.

7

Why Test

When I became a college teacher in the late 1960s, the revolt against traditional college teaching and testing was at its peak. A few years later, education analysts Samuel Bowles and Herbert Gintis published *Schooling in Capitalist America*, which argued that making students sit in rows and respond to questions regimented them, preparing them for regimented jobs on assembly lines and in cubicle offices.[1] Colleges used the grades resulting from tests to establish students' class rank, which local draft boards then used to determine which male students got drafted out of college to fight and die in America's poorly conceived war in Vietnam. Many new college teachers wanted no part of this process. When they became professors, some of my peers refused on ideological grounds to give grades. Indeed, entire colleges, from Evergreen State in Olympia, Washington, to New College in Florida, abandoned grades entirely. The grading function came to be seen as illegitimate—degrading, even (pun intended).

Since the primary function of tests had been (and still is) misconceived as providing a way to rank students, testing also became suspect. Some professors stopped giving finals or exams of any kind, instead relying on projects, term papers, and class discussion for evaluating student learning. Not giving tests also had a side benefit: Instructors then did not have to *grade* them.

Faculty members have long considered grading the bane of teaching. Some professors procrastinate on reading tests. Others minimize grading by giving only a single exam, usually at the end of the course. Still others use only multiple-choice exams that can be graded by machine—two hundred students in five minutes. And as with lecturing, many professors who do still test simply test the way they were tested. On autopilot. As if the pain of testing and grading cannot be confronted, only minimized.

All of this is a mistake. I looked forward to grading. Really! Grading is a voyage of discovery into the uncharted depths (or shallows) of your students' minds. It reveals what they know and don't know. It also reveals what you taught well and what you taught poorly (not that you are responsible for every wrong answer students make). Therefore, at a minimum, always grade at least some of your exams yourself. Doing so helps reveal ambiguities or other problems. If teaching assistants must grade some of your exams, be sure to debrief them about what students' answers are revealing.

Of course, tests are more appropriate in some courses than others. Testing is not the only way to give feedback to students; we should also comment on and grade their journals, projects, term papers, and participation in listserves and other electronic fora, as well as on class discussion, presentations in class, and so forth. But to throw testing out entirely is not usually thoughtful. Neither is relying too heavily on multiple-choice items. In most classes and for most students, avoiding testing, giving only a final exam, or resorting to multiple-choice tests amounts to bad pedagogy.

We must do better. Instead of falling into cynicism and easy excuses, professors *and students* need to look at testing as their ally in the learning process. Even grading can be your friend. And here's a key admission: *I feel so strongly about this that, in composing this book, I wrote this chapter first! Please, please let me persuade you that good testing is important and can improve—even transform—your courses.*

Seven Reasons to Test

We must start by considering: Why should we test? Many teachers and most students immediately think of one and only one reason for doing so, already mentioned: to evaluate student performance, in the service of awarding letter grades and other credentials. Moreover, it's evaluation for the sake of sorting and certification, not evaluation that leads to remediation or further learning. But evaluation is only one of *seven* functions that testing can and should play. You can decide which is the most important function.

A *second* function of testing is to convey to students that what they are learning is important. It would be great if all students saw the value of what you are teaching and were thus intrinsically motivated to learn it. Many students, however, don't see the value in learning anything on which they are not going to be tested. "Will this be on the exam?" they ask. If the answer is "No," then they infer they don't need to know it—hence it cannot be important. Testing conveys to students that your subject matters and that mastering it matters. I am convinced that testing is part of modeling and expecting excellence.

Third, tests prod students to keep up, to do the work for the course *as it progresses.* At many schools, this form of encouragement is sorely needed. Harvard University, for example, has an academic schedule that includes a "reading period"—the last week of each semester, just before the exam period. This dysfunctional nomenclature implies to students that they are *supposed* to do the reading for the course only during the reading period. All too many students infer that they need not do the reading before then. At many other colleges, some students get caught up in partying, drinking, student activities, or athletics and fall way behind. Some students simply cannot handle the freedom of having no high school teachers taking attendance and no parents overseeing what they do on school nights, so they do very little college work.

If a professor wants to hold informed discussions about the assigned reading during the semester, if they want students to work with other students to understand or apply the reading, even if the professor merely wants to ask in class, "Any questions about the reading?" then they have to resort to various measures to entice or persuade students to read as the semester moves along. As the preceding chapters on reading and course design have laid out, there are other methods to get students to read during the semester, but testing remains one of the more effective ways. Some students don't even realize how little they are doing, or rather, how little they are learning. They need corrective feedback early in the semester, not at its end.

Fourth, good tests cause students to learn *in the process of taking them*. Obviously, this function is enhanced when the exam is in an open-book or take-home format. But even an in-class multiple-choice question can prompt learning when constructed in the right way. Good essay test items help students make novel connections among different readings or concepts. They also give students practice in making summary statements of the gist of a reading or exercise.

Fifth, tests should cause students to learn *after* taking them, as they learn the right answer (if there is one) or discover how other students have replied with more depth and nuance. A related function is to provide feedback to students as to how they are doing, compared to other students and vis-à-vis your expectations. Tests can tell students their areas of weakness and strength. Students can also learn of and then remedy weaknesses in study skills (e.g., reading, highlighting, and annotating; understanding a table) as well as testing skills (e.g., writing and test-saviness on multiple-choice items). Again, it's critical to test mid-course, so you can help students develop study skills, get better at taking tests, and learn key content. If the only test in a course is a comprehensive final, these functions are lost; students learn they don't understand something only at the point when there is nothing they can do about it.

A *sixth* function is the mirror image of the fifth: tests provide feedback to the *teacher* about areas of student weakness. If most students show that they don't understand a topic, then obviously you have not covered it well. This is another reason to test as you go along. If an individual student shows a serious weakness, an early test can alert you so you can explore the difficulty, suggest or require additional help, and help the student fix the problem well before the semester ends. If a number of students show a serious weakness, you now know that you need to teach that topic again to help students improve their understanding.

A *seventh* function of tests is to prompt a review of the material covered thus far. This review can help students see relationships among the readings, discussions, and other course materials that they had missed. Reviewing can inspire students to ask interesting questions, either in class or during office hours. Questioning and discussing the material can help students organize the subject matter in their minds. The test can also signal to students what material is really important, worth testing. Research shows that reviewing after some time has passed increases retention. Reviewing coupled with integration (with other material from the course and from outside the course) is a major function of final exams and a reason to have finals. My students in Intro to Sociology have sometimes asked for a special evening review session; these were high-morale, high-intensity sessions that caused a lot of learning right before my eyes. (Study groups, by the way, can play a vital role in enlivening these review sessions.)

There are still other reasons to test, but I think these seven are the most important in terms of pedagogy. Most professors have not thought about many of them. However, understanding the functions that tests perform has implications for when and how one tests. Some of these functions surely relate to the course objectives you decided are important for your course.

Introducing Testing to the Class

It's a good idea to take the time to tell students (and especially TAs) about all seven functions that good tests fulfill. Doing so helps persuade students (and TAs) to buy into the importance of taking your tests.

And yet . . .

Students will still be tempted to ask, "Will this be on the test?" A good way to preempt this evergreen query is by asking students, "*Should* it be on the test?" Or, "What *should* be on this next test after reading X?" Then students are figuring out what is important about that particular reading (or whatever material you are examining), exactly the intellectual response we seek. Invite them to concoct and submit exam questions that they think are important. Reward any good exam item with discussion points, if you award those, or special credit. If you have TAs, they should be submitting questions every week, too. They can ask their sections to come up with questions, with each section agreeing on their best items. This can lead to fine intellectual discussions as to what makes for a good item.

If you don't have TAs, ask students to pair up to think/pair/share a good exam question. Each student should try to convince her peer *why* her question is a good one. Be sure to incorporate good items from students and TAs into your exams, particularly the in-class written exam. I have had students make up exam questions, then vote by section on their best question. Doing so meant they bought into the idea of the exam, that exams are good, that questions can be good (or bad). Through this practice, students will see testing's value and understand the expectations of the course in a tangible way.

You might also consider directly discussing why the timeless question of whether something "will be on the test" is anti-intellectual.

If you have assigned lots of readings, or even if you haven't but can break an assigned reading into lots of chapters, a useful review exercise is to ask students which item should be dropped from the upcoming exam, and why. At the least, the ensuing discussion will generate a lot of engagement because it was started by students. Surely you will gain some useful feedback about the reading and what students did and did not derive from it. They may then vote to reinstate that item and choose a different one. You can influence all this, subtly, of course, by guiding them to drop an item you didn't think was so central, or about which you didn't have any good questions anyway.

Other Ways to Make Testing More Meaningful

Before thinking about ways to make your tests more meaningful, you must think hard about them, especially when teaching new courses and/or using new items. If your *tests* are about stupid things, such as multiple-choice questions about unimportant "twigs" in your subject, then your *course* is about stupid things, such as those multiple-choice twigs (I call them "twigs" because they represent testing on minutiae rather than testing on the forest or even the trees, for that matter). If your course is about deeper, more serious things, then your tests (and the other things you grade) need to be about deeper, more serious things.

Flipping perspectives can also help. The first exam, for example, can be used to teach students how to *grade* an essay, which is key to learning how to *write* an essay. After the first exam, pass out three essays from previous years—A, C, and clearly awful—and have students evaluate them in pairs. This will help students turn in their own good essay next time.

Quantity of Tests

Test early and often.

Most professors do not test enough. Some believe that testing takes time away from teaching. Tests do indeed do that, but well-conceived tests can cause a whole lot of *learning*. If you think about it, surely learning, not teaching, must be our goal. Even the time students "lose" while taking an in-class exam can be a period of intense learning, to say nothing of the time spent preparing for that exam and then reviewing it afterward. Indeed, researchers Henry Roediger III and Jeffrey Karpicke found that "taking a test on material can have a greater positive effect on future retention of that material than spending an equivalent amount of time restudying the material." In particular, testing helped students retain information over the long term.[2]

Few courses should rely solely on a final. No evidence supports such practice as good pedagogy. On the contrary, research shows that students who are tested frequently retain more at the end of the course and also rate their classes more favorably.[3] You should do everything you can to avoid giving an exam that doesn't go back to students; instead, maybe do something else at the end of the semester—some sort of project or presentation that will get students thinking about your course long after the semester has ended. Final exam feedback, by contrast, rarely gets considered seriously by students. As a result, students may come away with off-kilter conclusions on final exams and leave your course believing them.

In these modern times, students have many options in terms of educational resources, including TED Talks, YouTube, and massive open online courses, or MOOCs, featuring nationally recognized lecturers; few professors can compete with these gifted speakers or rival the production values of these resources. So, what exactly do you as a professor bring to the table? Interaction with your students. This is your trump card. The most important element of that interaction comes from learning what and how your students think and know and feeding back to them evaluations about that, along with ways to improve. Without good testing, professors have little knowledge of what students know and can do, and hence little substance to give as feedback. Lacking that information, students predictably will find such a professor less interesting and less helpful to their learning.

8

How to Test

Unfortunately, many college teachers know little about testing. Most just use the same kind of in-class exam that they took when they were in college: a set of mainly multiple-choice, "identification," short-answer items, often with one essay question at the end.

Such tests suffer from several problems. The most significant of them is the pressure of the ticking clock. Although it follows a certain logic, the test's timed nature nevertheless rewards fast readers and facile writers. Different students manifest different strengths and weaknesses. Accordingly, your testing styles should also vary, giving various students various chances to shine. To be sure, reading fast and writing quickly *are* desirable skills, but they are not the *only* skills to be rewarded. Professors want to reward students who know more content, terms, and approaches relevant to their subject matter, but they can get misled by the surface skills of the fast reader and glib writer.

So, here is my general advice on testing in most college courses: I suggest that you have at least three tests in a semester-long course. The first should be a take-home test. The second can be a traditional, in-class, timed test—but a *good* one, which I'll show you how to construct. Then, your final exam should be *oral*, administered in small groups.[1]

This arrangement diversifies challenges and rewards. It also solidifies your conclusions about student inadequacy and non-mastery. You can be more confident that a student who cannot do good written work at home and in the library, even with open resources and plenty of time, who cannot perform in class under time pressure, and who cannot talk effectively deserves to get a poor grade.

Be careful in all this. Your syllabus should state that your tests are cumulative. Highlight that concept when you return the first exam by telling students that some material from this exam will return in the next and in the final. If there is an item that many students got wrong, at least in part, you may even consider including it unchanged on the next test. Also, point out to students some of the "takeaways" from the course thus far—principles, ways of understanding, maybe crucial bits of information—that they will want to retain five weeks hence on the second exam. You would be remiss if you implied to your class that they can now put away what they have "learned"—that it's done with.

Even with three tests, however—and three very different ones at that—tests should determine only part of a student's overall grade, usually less than half. The rest comes from their class discussion grade; their section or lab grade (if you have sections or labs); their project or term paper; small paper(s), book report(s), and journal; group project participation, if applicable; and any other components as listed in your course outline. Give letter grades on many of these tasks, too, although on journals I mostly give +, √, or -, partly to prevent students from feeling daunted by proper letter grades and partly to encourage them to write about what's really going in their minds.

Put a practice exam up on the website for the course, a week before the real one, especially if it's an in-class exam. Students will read it because you're doing them a favor by posting it, and that's exactly what you *want* them to do—read and think about problems connected with your course. Particularly on the first exam, and particularly if the exam is in-class, be sure to include at least one item from the practice exam verbatim, so students will not feel "gamed."

The first exam should be *a take-home exam* and should go out rather early in the semester, after at least one important unit of material has been covered. I "sell" it to students by telling them that the first unit contains terms and concepts they will need to retain for the rest of the course, so it's crucial to learn them now. "That's why," I tell them, "It's a test *to criterion*." That is, they have to take it until they pass it, as my written instructions, included below, make clear. Passing the exam is a prerequisite for moving on.

This is an example of "competency-based education," which posits that learning is often like stepping up a flight of stairs; it also starts your semester off right, by implying that your subject matter is important. It tells students that studying throughout the semester will be required, not just cramming at the end. And it puts you in touch with students who are doing badly early in the semester, rather than when it's too late to give them useful help. Because students have all the time and resources they might need, such a test obviates the need for special accommodations.

On the take-home first exam, grading to criterion means that you are not grading on the curve. Criterion grading is good pedagogy, as it emphasizes mastering the subject matter rather than competing against other students. Comments on a graded test (or paper or project) are for students to learn from, not to justify your letter grade. They particularly help students who have to retake part of the exam.

Even for a take-home exam, you can help students prepare. Suggestions in earlier chapters (about reading, writing, numeracy, etc.) are relevant here. Don't require your students to guess your expectations. Tell them how much or (perhaps more importantly) how little you expect in their answers. Sometimes students throw everything they can at an answer, burying a potentially coherent answer under verbiage. Perhaps you want them to show calculations. Perhaps not. Maybe you need direct textual support in answers. Tell students that you want them to refer to work by others, and explain how they should do it. Usually, take-homes do not require the elegant citation style you may require for term papers, but you do want students to refer to the course material and to signal you when they are doing so.

One useful strategy to teach students is to employ a line of argument that goes as follows: "Here are the two polar viewpoints on this issue, but I say . . . " For example, if a question asks, "What role does reward play in education?" the student should not just rush into her answer. Instead, she might begin, "X claims that differential rewards mostly get in the way of true learning," and then quickly summarizes X. She could follow that with, "But Y claims . . ." along with a summary of Y. Thus, she has shown that she has done the reading and understood it, and has set the stage for supplying her own position. Helping a class develop an answer in this form not only teaches them the form but also reviews the readings by focusing on at least two important viewpoints.

Usually, I give students most of a week to complete a take-home, handing it out perhaps on Friday and requiring it back (no excuses) the next Wednesday. When handing the exam out, I announce that I will answer any questions about it at the beginning of the next class and at no other time. This procedure also assures that most students will at least read the exam by the next class and that they will attend that class. Sometimes their questions reveal unintended ambiguities in an item, so the opportunity to ask them is important.[2] I also announce that absence on the day the exam is due is no excuse, so students shouldn't stay home because their exam is not done. The *only* allowable excuse would be a medical excuse for the entire take-home period.

I preface the take-home exam with these instructions:

> It's unusual to have a take-home exam with short-answer questions. I use this format as a tool for learning. It is possible for you to get every question in Part I correct, so that the first four weeks of the course are tied together into an integrated whole. Then, during the rest of the semester, I can take for granted that you know this material. If you score less than 80, you will have to redo the exam. If your resubmission earns a score of 90, you get a B for the exam; 80 gets a C. If you *still* don't score 80, you must talk with me and perhaps try a third time; now 90 gets a C. Thus, it's in your interest to take time and do a really good job the first time. You have control over the exam and the level of your performance, so this is your chance to begin the course with an A.

I then supply a second paragraph:

> If I were a student confronting this exam, I would answer all of Part I myself, then get together with another student

(or with my crew) and discuss the answers until we were sure we had them right. *Such cooperative work must be limited to Part I. The answers on the rest of the exam must be your own individually.* Of course, since Part II is the essay portion, I'll know instantly if you work with other students on your essays.

These instructions convey high expectations to students: You envision "A" work from each, and if they don't produce at least "B" work the first time, they will the second time (though doing so then will earn them only a "C"). Indeed, you will take exceptional steps, such as meeting with those few who did not meet the criteria the second time, to get them to meet the criteria. You are communicating that you care that they succeed.

Testing to criterion has additional benefits. It implies that what you have taught thus far is so important that you expect and require mastery of it before going forward. Since you are not grading on the curve, everyone can (theoretically) get an A (and definitely a B), but success will require work. That work can be with other students, in considerable part; students aren't in competition with each other. I encourage students to work together because doing so transforms at least some class members into teachers, and teaching material is the best way to learn it.

I include multiple-choice (more on this treacherous element below) and short-answer items on this exam, which might seem laughable, since students can surely study until they find the answers. It's okay if your take-home emphasizes basic facts, because you can then take students' knowledge of them for granted during the rest of the semester.

However, at least some of my multiple-choice and short-answer items are difficult and thought-inducing.

The first question on a test should be easy. This gets students writing and helps them avoid demoralization. Here is an example of an easy question on the take-home: "Define individual racism, institutional racism, and cultural racism, and give an example of each in your own words." This item I would put in the short-answer part of the exam, on which I allow collaboration. Why would I care if a student confirmed her answer with fellow students? On the contrary, such a discussion would only affix the three types of racism more securely in their mind, with more detail. Even a student who works alone need only refer to her notes on my lecture where I discussed the three forms of racism.

Here is an example of a harder item on the short-answer part of the take-home exam: "Which of these two novels—*Gone with the Wind* or *Jubilee*—presents a less racist portrayal of the Civil War and slavery?" Such a question requires not just articulating definitions of racism but using them in a coherent argument.

After such a generalizing question, I might then add a more difficult essay question on the second part of the exam, where students are supposed to formulate their own individual replies:

> Explain how each form of racism applies or does not apply
> to *Gone with the Wind*. (Be sure to make the distinction
> between a racist society, such as the slave South, and a
> racist book *about* that society.)

This exam format works. Most students are happy because they exit the process with at least a B. They also feel they know a lot, including what they learned from their resubmissions, if required. And to illustrate the value of the knowledge they've gained, I make sure to refer to ideas from the first unit often in the coming weeks.

Aftereffects of the First Test

Playboy magazine ranked the University of Vermont among the top five party schools in the United States during the time I was teaching there. Such a ranking would suggest a student body prone to cutting corners and perhaps not as focused on intellectual pursuits. Yet, after giving exams like this to hundreds of UVM students, I believe that I never encountered a single case of plagiarism.

Usually, about 10 percent to 20 percent of a large class (eighty or more students) score below 80 on the exam the first time, and in that case, I give them a new copy, circle the items on their original test that must be redone, and staple the two together. When grading multiple-choice items, I rarely indicate the right answer. Instead, I put an "X" next to errors. Students then must do a bit of work to learn the right answer, even if that merely amounts to asking another student. My hope is that such conversations do not simply go:

> **Bad student:** "What's the answer to #3?"
> **Good student:** "B."
> **Bad student:** "Thanks. What's the answer to #5?"

There's at least a chance that this will happen instead:

> **Bad student:** "What's the answer to #3?"
> **Good student:** "B."

Bad student: "B! How can B be right?"

Good student: [Explains why B is right.]

Such conversations are particularly likely to happen in discussion sections. For that matter, you should devote a few minutes of the larger class, right after returning the graded exams, to discussing any item(s) missed by many students. Select good students who got the item right and invite them to explain their answers. On essay questions, too, students can learn a lot from hearing another student read her really good answer.

Almost all students get almost everything right when they hand in the exam the second time.[3] Usually, I meet individually with the one or two who still score below 80, trying to see if they have a learning disability, need special help, or simply aren't studying. One way to do this is to pick an item to which the student gave a really bad answer. Ask her to explain her answer.[4] The student may simply admit she did not do the reading. In that case, ask if that behavior will continue. If "no," then explore what will change. Also explore what should be done to deal with the failed exam.[5] Since I have announced in the course outline that getting an acceptable grade (80) on the first exam is a prerequisite for advancing, I have set the stage to have no F's or D's in the course. I can demand that students take special steps at this point to make up their deficiency and meet the prerequisite. If you are not testing to criterion, then require students who score below C- to come to your office to see you for such conversations.

When I have TAs, special help can come from that quarter. Call the student in, along with her TA, and have the conversation suggested above. Some campuses have good help centers. If yours does, touch base there ahead of time to see what they offer, alert them that a few students are coming, and give them students' names and problems.

This way of using tests as a tool requires more than a little courage on your part. I think of it as tough love for those who need it most. So, for the student who is simply blowing off the course, I suggest she drop it immediately so she can focus on her other classes. This suggestion shocks some students into realizing they must shape up. Others take my advice and drop out, which helps both of us. The student exits the course without the millstone of a D or F and has more time to do better in her other courses. Meanwhile, I avoid the headache of trying to motivate someone who doesn't like the course and isn't interested in the material. Teachers have to be willing to deliver such bad news, in hopes (often justified, sometimes not) that it will make a key difference for the wayward student.

This take-home exam is an example of "mastery learning." It lets "slower" students put in as much time as they need to learn the material not only to criterion, but even to perfection. I use the term "slower" because proponents of mastery learning emphasize that 95 percent of all students can master even difficult material, given enough time and some instructional help.[6] This format is also fairer to students from diverse backgrounds (immigrants, racial and cultural minorities, first-generation college students, etc.) who might require more time on assignments. It also empowers all students because it treats them as professionals who can choose to devote as much time to this task as they wish or need.

Ask students to consider the amount of work they put in on the exam, including studying ahead of time, finishing the exam itself, and, for those who had to repeat all or parts of it, studying and writing parts of the exam again. How would they rank that work against the work of taking initial exams in other courses: Did it take more work? The same? Less? I'll wager they'll reply "more." Then ask if it was worth it—that is, did they learn? Finally, ask if you should have graded on a curve, giving roughly the same number of A's as D's and F's, the same number of B's as C's. Explain that that answer of "more" was the reason you awarded more A's and B's, not because you're an easy grader. Then segue into sharing your expectation that students will also work harder to prepare for the second exam than they do in other courses, and if they show they have learned a great deal, the grades will once again not be curved. Curved grading is antithetical to creating a supportive critiquing group.

Don't worry if no one flunks your first exam—you're looking for students to learn, not fail! Indeed, it's almost impossible for anyone to flunk your first exam, since students take it until they pass it. It's fine—ideal even—if everyone gets at least a B. That was the criterion, after all. For that matter, don't worry if every student gets at least a B for their course grade—they will have earned it! High grades are not a problem when they are earned.

Do my tests allow for ambiguity? Often, they do. Consider the Frazier/Herskovits debate mentioned back in chapter 6 over whether and, if so, how much, the massive traumas of American racial slavery disconnected enslaved African Americans from African cultural ways. Who, in that classic exchange, was right? Did slavery, as Frazier argued, blast its victims into a terrifying new situation in which what they already knew was of little use? Or did important African cultural habits persist, as Herskovits maintained, despite the radical shifts and assaults experienced by enslaved Africans and their progeny? Well, to some degree the best answer depends upon the circumstance—the context in which you're asking the question, for instance. Oftentimes, students are disheartened by the ambiguity: "Just tell us the right answer!" they may demand. Yet, in certain cases like this one, "both" is actually the best, most learned answer—and an answer that also explains the reason for the ambiguity is even more impressive.

On Multiple-Choice Testing

Multiple-choice testing has its place in college teaching and testing, but also deserves its infamy as a slippery slope to sloppy methods and shoddy outcomes. The two advantages of multiple-choice questions are that they (1) help you diversify the topical range your tests can cover and (2) can, if designed well, also simulate some of the real-world pressure of being asked quickly to summon one's internal knowledge of important technical details. But teaching well with multiple-choice questions always requires the teacher to think hard about how and when to incorporate this element. Below, I review the most important pitfalls.

Multiple-choice and short-answer items can distract from your learning objectives. Multiple-choice and short-answer items lend themselves to what I call "twig tests." Here is an example from a 1994 test of mine:

> Which term does Russell Means prefer?
>
> **A.** Native American
>
> **B.** Native indigenous peoples
>
> **C.** American Indian
>
> **D.** Amerindian
>
> **E.** Sioux

I should explain that Russell Means was a leader of the American Indian Movement. He had spoken twice at the University of Vermont, where I was teaching race relations. This question was on my in-class exam in my introductory level course on that subject. I had assigned his portentous essay, "Fighting Words on the Future of the Earth," as a reading in the course.[7] Even with those excuses, it's still a poor item. What's wrong with it?

First, when I looked over my exam in 2016, looking for useful items to include here, I was no longer sure of the right answer and had to skim "Fighting Words" to reassure myself. True, more than two decades had elapsed since I taught that course or gave that exam. Nevertheless, I had no business testing on something that was not important enough for me to remember twenty years later. Such a question could not have emanated from my basic teaching objectives, discussed in the introduction to this book, objectives that supposedly guided everything I did in the course.

If you are using a textbook, its publisher may supply multiple-choice test questions. Usually, these are twig questions, asking about factoids hardly worth remembering decades later. Make sure you test on the most important ideas in the course, not on minutiae.

Let me gently suggest that most multiple-choice items do not test on the most important ideas. And, despite real-world experts' common need for quick competence, choosing one correct alternative among five multiple-choice items is actually not a skill that people ever need, outside of a competitive test situation. This ultra-narrow skill does not help one mobilize co-workers on a project, discipline an errant kindergartner, write marketing copy, or replace a MacPherson strut in a car's suspension. Most other ways of testing *do* use (and can therefore help build) skills relevant outside the test situation itself.

So, how does one move from twigs to branches and roots in this area? One way of doing this is to write and choose harder multiple-choice items. Often, such deeper questions challenge students to think less literally about learned ideas. Here is one question I've used that exemplifies the difference:

> Each of the following statements accurately describes the treatment of slavery in *Jubilee*, compared to *Gone with the Wind*, with one exception. Indicate the *exception*.
>
> **A.** *Jubilee* makes slavery appear more racist than does *Gone with the Wind*.
>
> **B.** A racist treatment of slavery may make slavery itself look less racist.
>
> **C.** What is racist about *Gone with the Wind* is the fact that whites are shown always on top of the social hierarchy, Blacks always on the bottom.
>
> **D.** *Jubilee* is based on years of careful historical research.
>
> **E.** All of the above statements are true; there is no exception.

Here, in order to select the best answer, C, students have to think about more than one thing they've learned, and also demonstrate that they have gained some fluidity with the ideas being juxtaposed. Merely depicting an extreme hierarchy is not necessarily racist. That's a fairly advanced insight, and this question helps to make it both effortful and memorable.

Generally, I think the best way to write better, deeper multiple-choice questions is to force yourself to stay close to your own teaching objectives. What are you trying to accomplish with this one question?

Here, it might help to recall Benjamin Bloom's list of the six major types of cognition:

—Knowledge (memorizing or recognizing facts and terms)
—Comprehension (restating in one's own words)
—Application (making useful to a specific problem)
—Analysis (identifying and examining parts or components, comparing and contrasting, etc.)
—Synthesis (making new connections)
—Evaluation (judging quality, validity)[8]

Writing questions aimed at the last three types of cognition in this list will lead to assessments that simultaneously challenge and teach your students.

A major weakness of multiple-choice items is the tendency of test-takers afterward to remember the alternative they selected as true, whether or not it was the right answer. Unless you go over the test in a later class, true/false items are particularly likely to confirm wrong answers; researchers have found that students tend to remember false items as true.[9] That is a good reason never to use true/false items. My Russell Means item is even worse in that it provides four wrong alternatives and only one correct answer. I suspect that only about 40 percent of my students picked the right answer, "C." If so, then nearly two-thirds walked away having answered incorrectly. That's poor pedagogy.

Traditional testing theory gets this assessment strategy backward. It suggests that "distractors"—wrong alternatives—should be just that: they should "distract" students from the correct answer. If fewer than, say, 5 percent of your students answer D to an item whose correct answer is C, then some test-makers suggest replacing D with a "stronger" alternative. Strong distractors are a kind of trickery, however. They make sense only if you are trying to sort students so some will get worse grades than others. Sorting and ranking is not an important reason for testing in a course. Worse yet, tests constructed along these lines will *dis*-instruct content. That is, students will "know" and recall more *wrong* information after they take the exam than before, because plausible but wrong alternatives seduced their "vote."

Multiple-choice tests can also unduly reward reading speed. This bias can be so severe that it can mislead professors into giving much higher grades to verbally astute students than their understanding of the subject matter would merit. The way that multiple-choice items reward fast readers is not obvious to most students. In my first full-time teaching position at Tougaloo, many of my students were intimidated by the fact that I came to Tougaloo from Harvard, where I had taught as a junior faculty member and grad student. They *wanted* me to give them multiple-choice tests, thinking that that form of testing would ensure their inferior schooling in writing and reading would not wreak as much havoc upon their grades.

I came to realize that, on the contrary, multiple-choice items turn out to be much more affected by one's facility with words than essay items. Why does selecting D on a multiple-choice item prove to be a shallower measure of learning than writing a competent, well-organized essay from scratch? Largely, it's because the former relies inordinately on mere reading speed. Consider this "Sentence Completion Question" put out by the College Board in its book *Real SATs*:

> Despite their ____ proportions, the murals of Diego Rivera give
> his Mexican compatriots the sense that their history is _____ and

human in scale, not remote and larger than life.

A. narrow . . . overwhelming

B. focused . . . prolonged

C. vast . . . ancient

D. realistic . . . extraneous

E. monumental . . . accessible[10]

The purpose of the SAT is to predict first-semester college grades. According to the Educational Testing Service, "Sentence Completion Questions require a broad vocabulary plus the ability to understand the logic of sentences that are sometimes quite complex." We are to infer that these two attributes should correlate with first-semester college grades.[11]

Perhaps they do, but if so, the Diego Rivera item, like SAT scores in general, is unlikely to do this predicting well.[12] To the extent that it works at all, that's probably because it rewards reading speed, which it turns out varies enormously from person to person. Within a classroom of successful college students, some read five times faster than others. Such variation does not occur in most other common human endeavors, such as talking, eating, or walking.

An experienced test-taker knows to try filling in the blank with each pair of words in turn and asking if that makes sense. Perhaps the first substitution, "narrow proportions," might, although Rivera's murals were pretty big. But without a doubt there is tension between "overwhelming" and the later terms, "human in scale" and "not larger than life." So our student tries the next pair. In all, she reads the stem at least six times—a cumulative total of 180 words—before settling on E, "monumental" and "accessible," as the best choice. Slow readers read at about 100 words per minute, so this item may take her two minutes. A fast reader can average 500 words per minute, which works out to about twenty seconds to complete the item.

You don't want to privilege fast readers and facile writers. You want your questions to ascertain your students' growth in your discipline, in the subject matter of your course. Brevity should help ensure you are testing what you are teaching, rather than inadvertently rewarding reading speed. Multiple-choice items should have short stems and never more than five alternatives. There is no important reason to always have the same number of alternatives. Three is okay. An alternative that no one chooses merely adds words to read, rewarding fast readers. An alternative that does not review anything important is educationally useless. And even if you are careful to shorten your multiple-choice items, they will still be harder for slower readers. It follows that such items should not dominate your test.

As you might expect, the more effort students put into an answer, the more likely they are to remember it later. Writing answers—even short fill-in-the-blank answers—causes more long-term retention than merely circling multiple-choice alternatives or filling in bubbles on answer sheets.[13]

On the other hand, *good* multiple-choice items can prompt students to learn while taking the exam. One way to design such items is by having only one wrong answer, along with four correct alternatives. Then, four-fifths of the information that students read on the exam is correct. To the extent that reading helps remembering, this testing format ensures students have an increased probability of recalling this information years later. Moreover, it's easier as a test writer to come up with multiple actual effects or actual causes than multiple plausible wrong ones.

A common form of this kind of item is "all but one," as in the following:

> Each of the statements below about Native Americans in Vermont is true *except* one. Identify the exception, which is *false*.
>
> **Vermont's Native Americans:**
> A. left the state or died out in the eighteenth century.
> B. live mostly in the northwest part of the state.
> C. live mostly below the poverty line.
> D. get no services from the BIA (Bureau of Indian Affairs).
> E. are mainly Abenaki but are not recognized as a tribe.

I designed this item so students are likely to get it right. A is the answer (the wrong alternative). A moment's reflection should show them that A and any other choice *cannot* both be true. I intended this item to reinforce information in one of the readings, hopefully implanting in students' minds four different problems that *do* afflict the Abenaki people. At the same time, it underscores that they hardly disappeared long ago. If 95 percent of my students get it right, fine! Such an item exemplifies testing function number four—exams as teaching instruments.

Note another feature of the Abenaki item above: It is economical in its use of language. Its stem consists of just three words. Students will never have to reread it. Again, such brevity ensures you are testing what you are teaching, rather than inadvertently rewarding reading speed.

Easy items have other benefits as well. Getting items correct convinces students that they *have* learned something—and most likely they have!

On the take-home exam, multiple-choice items can play a positive role, too. For instance, you can ask students to find some information from the U.S. Census—say, the population of their college's city or town in 1950. The questions can be short, the answers specific, and in the process, each student will learn how to find the right census table and how to interpret it.[14]

In-class exams might include some multiple-choice items that have follow-up questions asking students to explain why they selected the answers they chose. You can then use this short essay to give partial credit if the student's reasoning merits it, or you can consider it an independent item like any other, to be given a full complement of points.

The Second Test Can Be an In-class Exam

You value your subject. You are eager to teach it to your students, and you want them to learn it and value it as you do. That's why your exams should reflect the importance of what you've been teaching all semester. If you are a history professor, earlier events from September you've covered should still be relevant as you move into October. If you're an English professor, surely meter and structure are still relevant to the poetry you are teaching later in the semester. Now is the time when allusions really kick in! So, every test should be comprehensive. The second exam should be an in-class exam that contains concepts already asked about in the first exam or from the first weeks of the course. (Such an exam may include multiple-choice, short-answer, and essay questions.) Assure this connection by relating some new material back to earlier concepts or by contrasting readings. If you don't, you imply inadvertently that students can clear out the first several weeks of the course from their synapses to ready that space for new material. In turn, that clearance implies that your material is not important once students have passed the exam on it.

Make the exam as clear as possible. Items should follow a logical sequence—perhaps the order in which your class took up each topic as shown in the course outline. That will remind students of the context of each item, which can lead to better performance. Remember, better performance is what you *want*. You're not trying to trick students into making errors; you'll be happy giving everyone A's.

There are other reasons to suggest a conventional in-class exam. Such a test *can* perform all seven of the functions that we want tests to fulfill: evaluating; conveying the relative import of certain material; motivating completion of coursework; learning while answering; providing feedback to students; providing feedback to the teacher; and motivating review and study. Certainly, it can certify that students are doing the reading and passing the course. Beyond that, conventional exams can be good at assessing students' performance in ways students understand, because they result in a letter grade comparable to those given to other students. Conventional exams do also convey to students that what they are learning is important, because such tests likely include questions on a variety of in-class experiences, lectures, and media. The exam also prods students to review the material covered thus far and to do the readings now rather than procrastinate. If you devote some class time to reviewing those items that many students got wrong, then students will likely learn after taking the exam. You too will profit from the feedback about areas of student weakness. This two-way feedback should take place well before the end of the semester, in time to do both you and your students some good.

What to Do During an In-class Exam

Your procedure for administering your in-class exam is important. Your decisions will communicate information and behavioral expectations to your students, intentionally or not. Therefore, it makes sense to consider those decisions ahead of time so you can be as clear in your expectations as possible. Introduce the exam succinctly and in a matter-of-fact manner. State that most students will probably do well on it, because it contains no surprises. Tell them, "If you think an item is confusing or ambiguous, come up and see me at once."

You should always take your own test, preferably while students are taking it. That way, you get a sense of whether it has time pressure. You learn what you can write on an essay question in ten minutes. Sometimes I have discovered a misprint or other mistake or realized that an item is so ambiguous that it will delay or mislead students. In that case, correct it at once to the class, out loud, and leave the correction on the board.

I have never heard of group work on an in-class exam. To ensure that students do their own work, refer to the rules you laid out on the first day of class, when you handed out your course outline. Maybe you used the Teddy Roosevelt quote I suggested in chapter 1: "Far and away the best prize that life has to offer is the chance to work hard at work worth doing." Your course is important; students need to learn what you've been teaching. Cheating subverts all seven functions of a test, so you want to underscore that you will countenance none of it. Your TAs must signal that they, too, expect no cheating.

One way to reinforce this expectation is to devote a few minutes to the underlying philosophy. I've found that cheating is much less likely to happen when students *like* a course, and when professors emphasize the important and intrinsic reasons to take it. When a course or a test is under-explained or is deemed important merely as another course credit, that encourages cheating. Form, again, also matters: Cheating is easier for students to rationalize when all the questions are multiple choice. Such a test is anti-intellectual in the first place, in that it emphasizes the credentialing function of testing, precisely the function that cheating fulfills.

On the day of the exam, don't be embarrassed to take the usual precautions: outlawing use of cell phones and laptops, asking students to forgo (or turn backward) brimmed hats, and so on. If your school's testing center has proctoring rules you like, consider adopting and citing these in your classroom. My first teaching job was at Harvard—a true mecca for cheating in the western hemisphere—so I learned early to put in place such safeguards, starting with a seating chart. If the class is large, quietly walk around occasionally. You want to deter cheating even more than to apprehend it. You can also print two different forms of the same test, changing the order of alternatives on multiple-choice items or even changing the order of the items themselves.[15]

A seating chart served me well when I gave my first in-class exam at Tougaloo. In introductory sociology, I had taught Freud's four stages of psychosexual development—oral, anal, Oedipal, and adult or genital sexuality—as part of my discussion of socialization to society's norms. It seemed obvious to ask this question:

> Freud's four stages of psychosexual development are (in order):
>
> **A.** _____
>
> **B.** _____

C. _____

D. _____

I was not prepared when three students, who happened to be sitting next to each other, all replied: "oil," "annual," "psychosexual," and last, a stage so rarefied that I personally have never reached it: "nonmanual!" While such blatant errors are rare (and appreciated in the professoriat), you may also want to check students sitting next to each other for similar error patterns on multiple-choice items. If you sense a problem, always photocopy a student's exam before returning it.

Help Students Prepare for the In-class Exam

Of course, the goal of college is education. You know that if students learn the material, they will do well and be better for it. However, many (most?) students have been conditioned by various forces to understand that the grades they receive are the most important thing. Even students who are not working very hard are anxious about grades. Many feel they have little control over them. You need to show them that they *do* control their grades. The take-home test to criterion does that. For the in-class exam, you need to give them pointers on how to study.

Tell students a lot about your upcoming in-class exam. Explain its form, that it has 100 points, and so forth. In class, give examples of exam questions. Have the class answer them on paper, first individually, then paired up, and finally calling on the pairs. If you decide to use some "all but one" multiple-choice items that ask students to identify the *wrong* answers, be sure to present one such question in class. Help them work through how to solve it. Show how you would rule out each alternative, then guess among the remainder.

If you plan to subtract for wrong (as opposed to blank) answers, explain why. Such subtraction should leave students neutral as to whether to guess or not, *unless* they can eliminate one or more alternatives. If you do *not* plan to subtract for wrong answers, then encourage your students to answer every multiple-choice item.

Encourage students to form study groups to prepare for the in-class exam. Also, schedule a special optional session, perhaps in the evening two days before the exam. These occasions can be surprisingly festive—popcorn is generally appreciated. At a residential college, many students will come. You can ask students some of the questions that TAs and students have handed in as possible exam items. Right answers can be rewarded with chocolates. Or you can ask questions in the *Jeopardy* format: Shout out a term or person or date and ask them to respond in the form of a question. For example, "Russell Means" might call forth "Who was an American Indian activist?" "Cognitive dissonance" might prompt "What is a psychological process that causes people to change their attitudes after they have changed their actions?"

Include at least one item from the real exam, just to reward attendees of the special session, though you may want to keep that detail to yourself. If you have TAs, their discussion sections before the in-class exam should be review sessions. You should choose this week to visit your weakest TAs' sections to ensure that they don't give out misinformation in the course of the exam review. Especially at commuting campuses, special sessions can present a problem in that some students will not be able to attend. But all can attend their regularly scheduled section meetings.

The Oral Final Exam

You were in college once. Think back on the exams you took. Can you remember them? Can you remember specific questions from those exams? Most people have a hard time remembering the exams, and specific questions have disappeared from the mystic chords of memory. However, with an oral exam, students may recall individual answers or comments weeks later, even years later.[16] That's a more likely result with an oral exam than with any answers on a written exam, and of course, *no one* remembers answers on a multiple-choice exam. Similarly, oral exams are learning experiences. Even if a specific answer is not remembered, students heard the correct answer. They cannot have that experience if they replied inaccurately on a written test.

Given the great impact an oral exam can have on a student's learning, this form of assessment should be an important part of your testing repertoire. Immediately, I can hear some of you objecting: I could never do that! I have too many students! But hold on. Suppose you have 125 students and four TAs. You can give the oral exam in five sessions, each with 25 students divided into groups of five, each group administered by you or one of the four TAs. The oral final will take less than an hour per session, so for the five sessions, you can give the exam in a total of five hours. You will have to spend an additional hour or so with your TAs to discuss problems and record their grades. But you will grade the oral exam as it takes place, so your total time expenditure, including grading, will be six or seven hours. That's far less than if you gave a "standard" two-hour exam consisting of fifty multiple-choice items and two half-hour essay questions, because grading the essays would take many more hours.

Below are the oral final's rules; I hand these out with the questions, on the same sheet of paper, printed on both sides.

> The final will be oral, in groups of six. I will seat you in a circle. Either I or a TA will then call out the number of a question from the list of questions below and on the other side. Someone will volunteer to give the "primary answer" to that question. If more than one volunteers, the person administering the exam will pick the first hand. The primary answer takes not more than four minutes. You can use a few notes to guide your answer, on a small card perhaps, but you may not read your answer.
>
> The person adjacent to the primary answerer will then supply a "secondary answer," with a two-minute time limit, adding whatever is required to complete a superb answer to the question. (If the primary answer is already complete and splendid, the secondary person would want to highlight the best points of that answer. This happens about once every two years.)
>
> Then the question is thrown open to the group for a free-for-all for additional ideas, criticisms of the first two answers, whatever. The primary and secondary answerers may participate in the free-for-all but should first allow others to play a role. The free-for-all will last about four minutes.

The TAs and I will rotate to new tables. Then we shall call another number, and the whole process repeats. Each student answers only one question at the primary level. Thus everyone will give one primary answer, one secondary answer (since each person will be seated next to a primary answerer), and two or more free-for-all answers.

If I were preparing for this exam, I'd prepare two-minute answers for each question and four-minute primary answers for at least three of them. This will minimize the chance that "your" question will get "stolen" by somebody else or won't get asked at all. Not every question will be asked. It follows that the last person will have to "volunteer" for the final question I select. Thus, it's in your interest to volunteer early for any question you're prepared to answer well.

Your grade will consist of your primary grade (counted twice), your secondary grade, and your free-for-all grade.

Students have complete control over their performance. They can memorize an answer, deliver one from notes and time it, or just bluff. It's their choice. I have had students volunteer for a question, then speak at high speed for three minutes and fifty-eight seconds, then stop, completely. I've also had students—very few, not even one every second semester—who rely on their intellect and reading to think up an answer on their feet. Their lack of preparation is painfully obvious.

To prep for an oral exam, compose one more question than the number of students in the largest group. For this example involving groups of six, you should create seven questions. Each is an essay question—thought-provoking and challenging. Print them out and give them to students in class about a week before your first testing time slot. In a sense, the final is a take-home.

Once in a while, students have tried to "game" the exam. They imagine that they can find out who is in their group and collude with them so that each prepares only one question on the primary answer level. But there are always more questions than students. If I call "number 3" and no one takes it, I do not then say, "Oh, well, then, number 6." Instead, I point out that the clock is ticking and we shall sit until someone has volunteered for number 3. If no one does, then at the end of the exam period, I'll grade everyone on the basis of what has happened, which would be disastrous.

Similarly, because there are more questions than students, after all but one person has volunteered for a primary question, the last student has to answer whichever of the remaining questions that I pose. Usually, I go over this protocol with students when I hand out the questions, so they understand that it is unlikely colluding will help them.

If you have TAs, they will be full partners in grading this exam, and they must be up to the task. Assign each TA to become expert on understanding one question—one with which they feel comfortable and which they will administer. Review their answer in your last TA meeting before the final—this makes for a great learning experience as other TAs chime in on points to look for.

Scheduling an oral exam in small groups has its challenges, but these are not insurmountable. Suppose you have thirty-five students. You can either form them into seven groups of five each or six groups of about six. Groups should never be smaller than four nor larger than seven. If you choose six groups of about six, then each group will take about sixty minutes, perhaps a little more, and you have to allow a few minutes of "downtime" at the end, to collect your thoughts and let students come in and out of the room. So you need to find six 75-minute periods for administering your exam. Usually, it's no problem to do two groups during the final exam period assigned to your class period. You can then schedule the other four periods on different parts of that day or on different days. I find it works well to offer different days. Some students are grateful to take your exam on an early day, perhaps because their other exams happen to be piled up later in the examination week, or perhaps because it means they can go home early. Others are grateful to take your exam on a late day, because their other exams are piled up early in the examination week and they can concentrate on your course after finishing their others.

Announce that the final exam questions will go out to students in their regular class a week before the exam period begins. Specify that date in your course outline, where you also describe the final. Before that date, you could put all six exam time slots into an email or a survey or have a calendar signup—whatever technology you feel most comfortable and capable with. Explain that the final will be oral, taking no more than seventy-five minutes. Ask each student to pick their first, second, and third choices of time slots. Invite students to choose times *other* than the two assigned time slots on the exam day, to leave room for classmates who cannot take the exam except in those slots. Then use their choices to assign them to groups. (Rarely have I had to assign students their third choice.) Then communicate to the students their assigned time slots and rooms.

Each TA must come to each session of the final, so before you choose the times for each session, you must know their schedules. For a class of 125 students with four TAs, you will need five small nearby spaces for the exam. These could be five small rooms, or perhaps you can use the four corners of your large lecture hall plus a nearby tiny room—maybe the stage. Put six chairs in a circle in each space.

When the approximately twenty-five students come to the lecture hall for the first exam, review the format for the exam. It is important to tell students (and TAs) that you or the TA leading each group will not speak as you normally do in class discussion, rewarding comments with little "um-hums" and nods. There are two reasons for this: You will be too busy jotting down the points just made, and you wouldn't want to mislead any student with a polite "um-hum" if the answer is veering offtrack. Suggest that when answering, students should speak to other students rather than to you.

Tell the twenty-five students and TAs that the secondary answerer will be seated to the left of the primary answerer. Then, divide the twenty-five arbitrarily into five groups of about five people each. Have them count off, or do it alphabetically; to prevent collusion, don't let friends stick together. Next, ask each TA to go to their exam group, as you go to yours. Each of you then seats the students arbitrarily, based on, say, their first names, in an alphabetical, clockwise order—again as a deterrent to collusion.

Unbeknownst to the students, each of the four TAs already knows which question they will call out—"number 3" or whatever. After the primary answer, the secondary answer, and the additional discussion, TAs move to a new group, as do you. And the process repeats. Because you have prepared six questions, this leaves two unassigned to TAs. Therefore, when you join a group, you will be able to choose between the remaining two questions with each group.

My oral exam tests aspects of life. It's reasonable to ask students to talk. Writing is not the only way people display what they know. Checking boxes is not even a *good* way for people to display what they know. Too often, professors give written final exams simply because *they* took written final exams. Perhaps the silliest example I have seen was a written final exam announced at a college in New York City for a speech class! In assessing students through the oral exam, I am able not only to see what they have learned but also assess them in a way that teaches them valuable skills, and in a way that will stay with them, in some form or other, for quite some time.

A word of caution: On oral exams, you will want to avoid provoking test anxiety. When I first used oral exams, I deliberately *raised* anxiety levels for the oral final. I worried that students would not take it seriously, would rely on their ability to speak well, and so forth. Just the opposite occurred: One student threw up before the exam!

Because you want students to keep on learning about the subject after the course is over, you might consider a question on the oral final exam that asks, "What are the main issues that this course did not get to? What do you think are some answers or insights regarding those issues?" Or, in a literature course, "What would you read next? Why?" In the oral exam format, this can generate a fascinating discussion.

Doing Better with Testing

The lazy assumption that testing is merely a means of imposing arbitrary grade schemes on hapless students is a central element of the compact of complacency that continues to hamper college teaching and learning. Properly planned and utilized, tests are actually a major—and increasingly underused—tool for achieving what ought to be the true and best goals of higher education. If we want to live up to our potential as college teachers dedicated to developing the potential of all our students, we will have to think seriously about how we can creatively challenge our students through assessments. The time spent taking a test should be at least as interesting as any other part of your course. As teachers, our job is to make assessments interesting and full of purpose. To do anything less is a disservice to our students, as well as to ourselves.

9

Grading

The final piece of assessment is of course the grade. For some of your students, that is what they'll want to see and what they'll remember. For you, it's likely the least important part of assessment. You might feel some pressure in ascribing a grade to a work, for a multiplicity of reasons. Don't "play God" in grading! That is, don't give students grades they do not deserve, either inflated or deflated, hoping to prompt better future performance.

When dealing with a student who has done poor work all semester, a professor may give a barely passing paper (and "give" is the operative term) a B– instead of the C– it deserves, hoping to encourage better work from the student in the future. Unfortunately, the B– too often tells the student that mediocre work is all that is required for a B–. Alternatively, when dealing with a student who seems very capable but has done B– work all semester, a professor may give an average paper a C– instead of the B– it deserves, hoping to stimulate the student to do better work. Unfortunately, the C– may convince the student that you don't grade fairly, especially if she compares her essay with others that got better grades.

And don't forget that we have entered the age of easy, instantaneous information sharing. Your grades may very well get seen widely and very quickly. Students have always compared grades; today, they may even set up private Facebook pages or other social media about your course. You had best be able to justify your grades, which you cannot do if they have an element of God-playing in them, even if the distortion was done with the best of intentions.

Not all writing needs to be graded or corrected. You can require writing in class, perhaps a reaction to a lecture idea, and *not* correct it or grade it but just respond to its content, perhaps during class discussion, perhaps individually. Don't grade down for composition flaws on an in-class task or exam, unless they impair the substance of the answer. (They probably will, though! Or they will at least lessen the credibility of the answer.)

Numerical Devilries

Most professors aren't proficient in statistics. As a result, they often construct exams that unintentionally overemphasize precisely those parts of their exams that prioritize verbal acuity over content knowledge. Consider this common exam format: fifty multiple-choice items, each worth a point, and one essay question, worth 50 points. The professor may then think he is grading students equally on two very different skills: filling in answer bubbles and writing a coherent essay. He is aware that the first skill will never be useful once students have graduated to life and the workplace, but he rationalizes that letting half of their grades be determined by a machine lets him devote more time to grading the essays.

But an undesirable aspect of multiple-choice test sections is that they can unreasonably over-penalize students. Unless a student leaves an essay question blank or puts down a blatant joke or a wholly unrelated response, a less than satisfactory answer to an essay question can still earn its author 60 or maybe even 70 percent of the possible points. A student may struggle to effectively communicate their thinking in an essay, yet their level of effort is an inherent criterion that we often acknowledge through our essay grading. More often than not, we do not give a failing grade to essays when we see a reasonable attempt has been made—even when their attempt is not successful. So the lowest scores on the essays generally won't be so low—maybe D's and D-'s. Not good, but not disastrous to a student's average.

There is no such "At least I went through the motions" floor beneath a student's feet on multiple-choice segments. A less than satisfactory performance here is an F—the machine graded it and there it is. Doing a little better than guessing might earn a student a 20 out of 50, for example. A terrible performance can yield scores far below 50 percent of the available credit—effectively a sub-F grade component. So, when each section is weighted equally, the multiple-choice section—often the lower-level critical thinking portion of the assessment—can pull a student's grade down disproportionately. A poor effort on the essay is not going to damage a student's overall average as much as a poor effort on the multiple choice. If your students realize this, they would be smart to spend more time considering the multiple-choice questions and less time on the essay—just what you don't want! This isn't a reason to renounce all multiple-choice testing, but neither is it something to ignore.

Examining assessment results teaches us about student learning and our own effectiveness. A simple alternative to the disproportionate influence of different kinds of assessment is to weigh them differently.

Ultimately, one should always ask: What do my assessments and grading practices communicate about what I most value in my class?

What about short-answer items? For example, this question from my race relations in-class exam:

> *Explain the difference between acculturation and syncretism.*
>
> (4 points)

For an answer to get four points from me, it had to be excellent. A "merely" good answer got three points. An answer that showed some knowledge but had serious problems got two points. Now consider: Two points out of four is equivalent to 50 points out of 100, and a grade of 50 out of 100 is a low F. I did not mean to give students an F when I gave them two points on their short answer. I was just using the few points available to me on the scale to differentiate among answers and communicate to some students that their answers needed work. I meant for two of four points on this item to roughly equate to a B– or C+. So, short-answer items will wind up being weighted, de facto, even more heavily than multiple-choice items. A good way to deal with this problem is to award fractional points.

When grading multiple-choice items, be sure to subtract a fraction for wrong (as contrasted to blank) responses. Not making this subtraction is, I think, anti-intellectual. Here's why:

Suppose you have a hundred multiple-choice items. (That would be terrible testing and terrible pedagogy, but it makes for easily understood statistics, so bear with me.) Suppose one of your students, Suzie, barely attended class and did not study for the exam. Therefore, she does not read any item, but she does answer them all, filling in the little bubbles with her pencil. If each item has five answers

("A," "B," "C," "D," and "E"), then on average, Suzie will get about twenty correct.

Ernie, on the other hand, reads very slowly, but he is diligent and has mastered the material. At the end of the fifty-minute exam, he has trudged his way through only twenty items, but he got them all correct.

If you don't subtract for wrong (as opposed to blank) answers, Ernie and Suzie will get the same score—20! Yet they are very different students and have performed very differently.

You can try to fix this problem by suggesting to all students that they should guess if they don't know the right answer, "because nothing will be taken off for wrong answers." Data show, however, that many students will guess only for those items about which they are unsure. But Ernie encounters no such items. So that kind of advice will not solve the problem.

What Ernie should do is answer nineteen items, getting them all correct, and then use his last two minutes to go "B," "B," "B," "B" all the way down the answer sheet. If he does so, on average he will get one-fifth of the remaining eighty-one items correct, or sixteen or seventeen items, plus the first nineteen, for a total score of 35 or 36, far better than his original score. So you could simply tell students to do this.

Few teachers if any render this advice, however. I think that's because marking "B," "B," "B" all the way down the answer sheet is anti-intellectual. Even if you bring yourself to tell them to do so, this will actually offend some students precisely because it's anti-intellectual. Such advice prompts students to think of your testing as merely a game, something they should try to "beat"—exactly the opposite of how you want them to think of tests in your course!

To treat testing as a game ignores every benefit tests can provide except the certification function, and even that one is trivialized under this approach. Moreover, the students most offended are often precisely those who care the most about education and ideas. Vocationally minded students are also put off, since they infer that the point of your tests is to game the system and score well, not to learn skills and knowledge that might actually be of use. Only the shallowest members of the collegiate subculture will be happy—and only because they will imagine that they can collect points just by chance in your class.

All these issues disappear when you subtract for wrong, as opposed to blank, answers. (And while we are discussing the statistics of grading, please heed this admonition: The old tale that changing an answer is bad because students usually change from right to wrong has no basis in fact.) How much do you subtract? The answer is simple. For each wrong answer, subtract $1 / (N-1)$, where N = the number of alternatives. Here, with five alternatives, you will subtract 1/4 point for each wrong (as opposed to blank) answer. Let's return to the Suzie example. Now, under the new rubric, the computation for Suzie's test score will be 20 (for her number of correct answers) - 1/4 points multiplied by 80 (her number incorrect), or 20 - 20 = 0. Her score of 0 is appropriate, since she did not even read the items. Ernie, on the other hand, will get a score of 20 (20 - 0 = 20), substantially better than Suzie, which again is appropriate. He has shown that he knows some stuff. If he instead followed the "B," "B," "B" strategy, he would get, on average, a score of 19 (19 + 20 - [1/4 points times 80] = 19).

Now, under this scoring method, you can honestly tell students that it makes no difference whether they guess or not. Guessing will neither help nor hurt them. Actually, you can (and should) encourage them to guess when they can rule out one or more alternatives as clearly wrong. If, for example, they have narrowed the correct answer down to either "C" or "D," then they should guess randomly between those alternatives. If they have done good work—if "A," "B," and "E" really are wrong—then random guessing will net them 1 point half the time. Again, a positive result is appropriate because they do show some knowledge.

It is also possible to use multiple-choice items as writing prompts. One way to do this is to ask students to provide an explanation of their answer directly below at least one multiple-choice item that they find unclear or are hesitant about answering. A good explanation can earn them half credit or even full credit. Of course, if they get it right, they automatically get credit for the option they marked, but you could offer bonus points, too. (Conversely, if they give bad information to explain a correct answer, then a poor explanation could cause them to lose some credit for their right choice.)

Your students' tests should be a source of your learning, too. Here is where you can find out how well you taught a concept or skill, and where students reflect back to you what they have learned in the course, which may be quite different from what you think you have taught!

But here too is another drawback of multiple-choice exams, which is that they don't give you, the instructor, nearly as much information as other types of assessment. Teachers *do* get feedback on multiple-choice items when they note the alternatives that drew many erroneous replies and think about why. But that requires some guessing on the part of the instructor, because the only information available to them is in a small bubbled-in circle. Again, you might ask students to explain their thinking on some multiple-choice items that many got wrong. This conversation will help you to see where the students' thinking went wrong and how they arrived at their incorrect answer.

Still, multiple-choice items offer one major reward to professors: They can be graded by machine. Even if they grade them by hand, grading is much faster. They are not tasked with trying to make out semi-legible handwriting by students who are writing at breakneck speed. A machine can grade two hundred exams, each with a hundred different items, in ten minutes. Usually, it will also spit out diagnostics telling you the number or percentage of correct responses to each item right and the number or percentage of "voting" for each wrong alternative. You can then spend your time thinking about the results—examining those items that most students missed, judging whether some alternatives may have been ambiguous, choosing which questions merit in-class review, and deciding whether to call some students in for conferences in your office about their bad (or good) performance.

Multiple-choice items appear to offer another reward: They seem to be "objective," hence fair. Yet, as I've said, multiple-choice items may indeed be biased. But at least their grading is not. You cannot grade non-white students higher (or lower) than they deserve; you cannot subconsciously prefer women (or men). The numbers are what they are. Multiple-choice items also eliminate more subtle forms of subjectivity: Even if you *like* a student or are impressed by her, you will not read more into her answers than into the same answers coming from someone else. Nor will you subjectively read *less* into her poor answer on a different item owing to the "halo effect."

Principles of Grading Exams and Papers

Exams and papers are never just mechanisms for evaluating your students' performance. They should ideally be forms of communication between you and your students—the students can show you what you have been teaching, and you can use their work and your feedback to let them see what they've learned and what they still need to learn. Therefore, it's your responsibility to keep that line of communication open and clear.

To understand exactly how your students are performing well and where they are stumbling, do your own grading! In Canada (and probably elsewhere), professors hire grad students *not in the course* to grade! However munificent this convenience may feel to you, it still unavoidably deprives you of important information about what the students learned. Yes, you can ask your graduate student TA to report back, but what quality control is there? This is information you simply can't forgo. If the number of students permits, *you* should grade the major essay. Then there is more consistency in the assessment. If there is too much grading to handle alone, ask each TA to come to a meeting with representative samples of A, B, C, and D graded tests. Would you give those tests the same grades?

As you grade, take notes regarding what to teach in class when you hand back the exams, and put notations into your course notes as to what you need to teach better.

Never be late grading and returning exams and papers. Do not procrastinate. No test can fulfill its various functions if it does not get graded and returned students in a timely fashion. You should discuss the exam in the very next class meeting. Doing so requires planning.

If you have eighty students in a course and are going to get their responses to an exam on Tuesday morning, then you need to set aside extra time on Tuesday afternoon and Wednesday for grading. Adjust your schedule ahead of time. For example, if you routinely protect Wednesday and Friday afternoons for your professional writing, then switch Wednesday's writing session to the previous Monday. Otherwise, you may feel frustrated that grading is taking away from "your time" and go into the task already upset about it. If you have TAs, allot time for discussing the exam with them in section that week.

As you begin to grade an exam or paper, think about what students need to know. Don't comment on every error. That's reverting back to the "twigs" mentality of assessment. Students can figure out many of the right answers on their own. Invite them to compare their work with other students, to speak with their TAs, or to come see you, if the question is a big enough one. Instead of picking out each and every problem, give feedback on the main skills and main ideas that students conveyed well or poorly.

Always grade tests blind. When you read an essay or even a short-answer item asking for a sentence-long response, you should not know who wrote it. It's a simple matter to have students write their names on the back of the exam, not the front.[1] You also want to grade each new page blind, to avoid any halo effect, positive or negative, stemming from responses on the previous page. A student may answer an essay so brilliantly as to blow you away, convincing you she can walk on water. You may then grade her *next* essay too leniently, inferring scintillating perspicacity where merely solid insights abide. That's a positive halo. Conversely, if your test consists of fifty multiple-choice items followed by a long essay, you may be unfairly harsh with an essay from a student who got an abysmal score on the multiple-choice part.

Her bad performance on the multiple-choice items has already damaged her score enough; it should not spill over to hurt your evaluation of her possibly better performance on the essay question. So, after finishing the multiple-choice part of the answer sheets, fold them over so they cannot influence your evaluation of the rest of the exam.

As you grade, reflect on what you are reading. Read several essays to get a sense of what students are thinking, writing, and how they are doing. Doing so allows you to understand what you have taught well and what the students have learned. Put temporary grades on the essays. Try to connect these with a rubric, if appropriate. Be open to replies different from what you had expected. This practice can inform your framing of the assessment when you return it to the students.

I usually triage questions in the post-exam debrief session. Those that most students got right are not worth discussing in class or discussion section. Some other items may not be worth discussing because most students *should have* gotten them right, in which case the students will be able to figure out the right answer (whether multiple choice or essay) on their own. A second group of questions, missed by some students and in specific ways, leads logically to short discussions by TAs if you have TAs, or a quick give-and-take in the whole class if you don't. Just ask, "Who got number 11 correct and knows why?" Then call on one of the raised hands for an answer, followed by, "Any questions?" Or, for a question you don't want to discuss in class, ask those who got it right (or who got 90 percent or more on it, if it's an essay item) to raise their hand. Suggest that others ask to see these students' answers and also get advice about their own answer. You can also encourage those groups or pairs that worked together on the take-home test to reassemble after this exam to deal with wrong answers and compare grades and comments on essay items. If a group concludes that an answer I gave is *wrong*, they can compose a written appeal making their case.

Finally, most of the class may have missed a few items. These you need to address in the larger class (unless your TAs have a firm grasp on them). Usually, addressing these items will lead to good, short corrective discussions. Again, you can start those discussions by calling on a student who got it right.

Some items may have been harder for the students than you anticipated. Consider this axiom: If fewer than 20 percent of your students answered a multiple-choice item correctly, it is a bad item. It means that a lower proportion got it right than would have been expected by chance. Such an item has "misbehaved," and scores on it should be dropped from overall exam scores. If each item is worth two points, give every student two points for that item. Then teach it better![2] Students will appreciate your fairness and see that you are committed to their success, not to trying to get them to fail.

Not only should you not be trying to fail students, but you must also recognize they are responsible for their successes. When discussing grades (on an exam or for a paper, project, their participation in discussion, or the course overall), never say, "I gave you a B." Always say, "You earned a B," or "Your essay was of B quality." Stay focused and help students stay focused on learning the material, not arguing for the grade. To students, grading can be kind of a mystical process handed down from on high. Remove the opacity by sharing a good answer with the entire class, explaining why it's a good answer, and congratulating those who had an excellent response.

Some professors find that students are more interested in their grade than in the comments they receive, even to the point of not reading the comments. Research shows that many pieces of feedback from professors are not even well understood by students.[3] When you hand a test back to a student who did not do well on it, or when a student complains to you about a grade on a test (or term paper or project or whatever), ask them, "Are you proud of your work?" I suspect they won't say they are. Ask them to write down a sentence explaining why their answer is a good one. Using that sentence as a focal point, help the student understand what you expected of them. They might be able to help you understand why their answer was actually better than you had originally judged it!

If you wish, you may want to use your first exam to spark class discussion about testing and grading. Students and TAs can use their knowledge of the seven functions of testing to critique your first test, which will be valuable to you when you compose your next one.[4] There are additional ways to use your test to spark discussion. Before handing it back, ask students to predict their test grades and to estimate their effort, on a scale of 1 to 10 (with 10 being the highest). Then hand back the exam and have them compare their predicted and actual grades. It can be interesting to ask for a show of hands from students who predicted their letter grade exactly, within a + or -, or failed to predict it.

You can invite students to call out the aspect of the exam that was their biggest disappointment—that is, the part on which they got a bad score, to their surprise. Do they understand why? If not, they can discuss it with either their TA or you. Students can report the results in a journal entry, if they are keeping a journal for the course. Alternatively, you could also have them give their answer and invite other students to critique it and point out what is missing.

Another productive discussion of test-taking involves sharing with students three essays from previous years, their names removed—ones that you graded "A," "C+," and "D–" or "F." Spell out the criteria or show the rubric that you used to reach these decisions. You are thus teaching them, "Here is what I value in an answer." Don't tell them which essay received which grade. Ask students to grade all three and include short comments. Then ask the entire class to share their grades. I predict you'll find that most students graded as you did. If you don't want to devote class time to this, students can also do this exercise in their journals, though covering it in class usually generates an upbeat and interesting discussion. The payoff is that students develop an understanding of what a fine essay in your field looks like. (For all these exercises, I suggest using exams and papers from previous years to remove any potential embarrassment or shame on the part of students who received poor grades.)

After handing out the first exam grade, send an email to every student who got below a C–, and maybe to others who you think underperformed. If they have spoken in class or otherwise shown some work, express your disappointment in their performance, your belief they can do better, and your willingness to meet with them (or they can see your TAs if you have a big lecture class). Often, they've never received an email from a professor before, and it can nudge them toward doing something about their grade. Example:

> Your score on the second exam wasn't as good as I expected. Since it's still early in the semester, now is the time to try and figure out what went wrong and how we can fix it. I have some quick questions for you that I'm hoping you'll be willing to answer for me.
>
> First and most importantly, do you know why you didn't do well on the exam? Did you read the material

(and mark it up)? Did you come to class and participate in the discussions on a regular basis? Do you have a study group? Would you like to come to see me in my office hours to discuss the material?

With this information we can figure out what happened and work together so that the rest of the course goes more smoothly!

Grading on the Curve

It's your course, but I hope I can convince you that grading on the curve is not good pedagogy for a number of reasons. Grading on the curve, for readers with the good fortune not to have encountered it before, means that a professor calculates numeric scores on every student's test before assigning letter grades. Then, based on the distribution of those scores, the professor figures out what letter grades to assign to which numeric scores. True, grading on the curve helps you identify gaps in performance, through which you can establish the difference between, say, an A and a B. Researchers understand one of the major problems with grading on the curve is that having grades fall within a "normal" distribution is not a sign of rigor, but a sign that too many students were not taught well.[5] As professors, we should actually be ecstatic to have all of our students score A's! We, too, though, like our students, have been somewhat conditioned to understand grades as a zero-sum game—some students have to do poorly and some have to do well. This isn't true, though—you can still be a demanding grader and have students do well. And panic about grade inflation is a hoary old trope, as evidenced in this advice from a report of the Committee on Raising the Standard at Harvard University, published in 1894: "Grades A and B are sometimes given too readily—Grade A for work of no very high merit, and Grade B for work not far above mediocrity. One of the chief obstacles to raising the standards of the degree is the readiness with which insincere students gain passable grades by sham work."[6]

My own view is that grade inflation is probably happening, but there are good reasons to stay both calm and critical about this. The evidence is complicated, contradictory, and quite interesting—certainly worth tracking. Interestingly, Clifford Adelman, a senior research analyst with the U.S. Department of Education, actually did analyze past and present data on grade inflation, reviewing transcripts from more than three thousand institutions and reporting his results in 1995. His finding then was that grades had actually declined in the previous two decades. Later studies showed no grade inflating in the nine years following Adelman's report.[7]

My own long experience confirms that, if your grading is perceived as fair, then students do not need high grades to give you good course evaluations. I got good course evaluations even though my courses were considered hard, at both Tougaloo and at the University of Vermont. A 2018 study confirms that my experience holds true with other professors at other institutions.[8]

Grading an In-class Exam

The three-test regimen I propose—the take-home first exam, the in-class exam, and an oral final—allows consideration of curved grading only on the written in-class exam. Most professors grade such exams at least a little bit on a curve, and that's okay. Doing so allows them to be flexible as they consider student performance. Your exam is largely new, we hope, not a copy of last year's, and you cannot be certain how students will perform on a new test.

However, imagine a test on which thirty students score as shown in figure 1. If you had decided ahead of time that a score of 90 was required for an A, 80 for a B, and so on, then you would have five A students, twelve B's, eight C's, four D's, and one F. That might be fine with you and appropriate for your students, which is what counts. Determining what is appropriate for your class comes down in part to a gut feeling. If your students have been doing a good job discussing the reading, lectures, and other course components in class, if they seem to have learned a lot, maybe awarding only five A's does not sufficiently recognize their accomplishments. Test items can be harder than anticipated.

How would you group the results in figure 1 for the purpose of assigning letter grades?

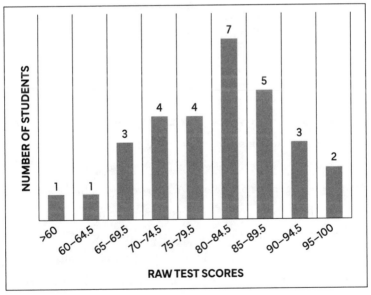

Figure 1: Numerical Scores on Exam 1

When I went to college, teachers often plotted a distribution of the grades similar to that depicted in figure 2.

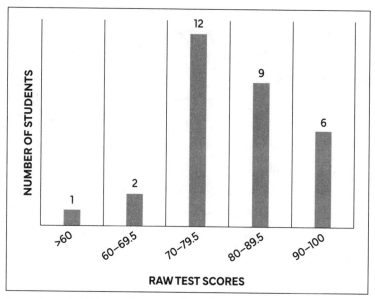

Figure 2: Possible Distribution of Grades on Exam 1, 1960

More students got A's than F's, but grades clustered around B-. Recently, though, things have changed. Perhaps owing to societal pressures, or perhaps owing to the changing expectations of both students and professors, it seems now that "A" is by far the most common grade on both four-year and two-year college campuses (comprising more than 42 percent of grades). "At four-year schools, the awarding of A's has been going up five to six percentage points per decade, and A's are now three times more common than they were in 1960."[9]

In light of what many perceive to be rampant grade inflation, professors today may desire a grade distribution like that depicted in figure 3.

You may wish to choose different dividing lines for the different grades, thus yielding outcomes where perhaps 35 percent of the

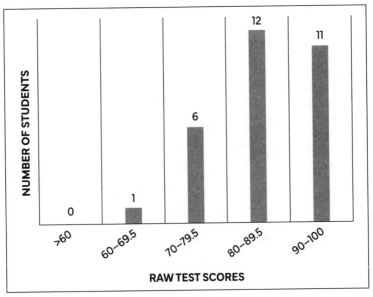

Figure 3: Possible Distribution of Grades on Exam 1, 2023

grades are A's, 40 percent B's, 20 percent C's, and just 5 percent D's and F's. But the process is still the same: What constitutes an A is not clear until after the results come in.

What if your class is exceptional? Every veteran teacher has had a class that performed better than others. Is it appropriate to give only 35 percent of *those* students' A's? Maybe the proportion should be 70 percent! Or what if your class disappoints you? What if you sense that they have not studied much and are not taking the course material seriously? Is it appropriate to give 35 percent of *those* students' A's and 40 percent B's? Conversely, in a weak class, maybe only 15 should get A's, and maybe a full 30 percent should receive warning shots across their bows in the form of D or F grades on their first exam.

Some individual test items may have been harder than you anticipated. Again, remember the axiom that if fewer than 20 percent of your students answered a multiple-choice item correctly, that is a bad item, and every student should be given credit for that item.

On the second (in-class) exam, you should therefore have some flexibility in setting what is an A. As you record numerical grades, always keep track of what constitutes an A (and an A–, B+, etc.). Then, when you give letter grades for things like discussion, or section participation, or projects, you can translate those back into numbers, based on the normal rubric where 90–100 = A, 80–90 = B, and so on. After that, you can make up a scale for semester grades that will be easy, after you add up all the numerical scores for each student (perhaps after dropping one grade, as mentioned in an early chapter). And, of course, leave room for fudging at the end, at least for fudging upward.

In my experience, the mixture of essay questions and more difficult multiple-choice questions and short-answer items will provide plenty of spread in students' scores. Indeed, I have found the top 10 percent of a 0–100 numerical scale to sometimes be not very useful. For one reason or another, even fine students miss some multiple-choice items. Short-answer items rarely provide for a score such as 4.5 out of 5, so few students score 90 percent on them. There is no sacrosanct rule that 90 percent must constitute an A. On some exams, 64 may be the highest grade in the class, in which case 60 percent correct may indicate exemplary performance. Nevertheless, students may not feel that you have taught well or they have learned well when they get a numerical score of 61, even if "A" is attached to it.

If a student has an uneven in-class exam, do give praise for what they did well. But don't soften the message that the student needs to improve their performance. As with the first exam, don't put up with a truly bad performance from any student. Meet individually with those who got D's or F's and explore their worst answers to understand their thought processes. Again, if you have TAs, get them involved.

Grades tell students how they are doing vis-à-vis other students. You should help illustrate this to them by providing a rough distribution of their grades. For some who do very poorly, if it's not too late to drop your course, suggest that option. Students need to know if they have a talent for the field or should avoid it, for example.

Altering Grades

Don't change students' grades. The grade they get is the grade they earned. Once in a long while, you may want to give a student a bit more than she earned, as a carrot, if you know she has been trying really hard and you sense that a little reward will lead to still more effort. However, never decrease a student's grade for any reason (unless, of course, you discover that she cheated).

10

Teaching Diverse Students

College populations in the United States have changed a great deal—though certainly not enough—over the last hundred years. When I was an undergraduate at Carleton in the early 1960s, women students were a distinct minority, both nonwhite students and international students were almost entirely absent, differences in gender and sexuality were neither acknowledged nor accommodated, and there was no such thing as the Americans with Disabilities Act. All of that has, of course, changed for the better.

With the growth in community colleges, more people than ever are going on to higher education. In concert with this change in student population has come great innovation in teaching and pedagogy. Fewer and fewer classes consist of hundreds and hundreds of students in an auditorium mutely attending a lecture. The advent of student opinion polls on campuses has caused professors to be more concerned than ever with their own performance, and, hopefully, more concerned about creating classrooms where each student learns and performs well.

But this raises the question of how we ought to do this. And on this topic, this book is intentionally cantankerous: I'm acutely aware that what I'm proposing in this little volume will be seen by some as flying in the face of recent drives to increase diversity, equity, and inclusion. I hear you, critics: "Just as we are trying to open our doors wider, here comes the white, male, cisgender James W. Loewen arguing that we need to work harder, raise our expectations, and give more tests! How does that help create new pathways for disadvantaged students?"

I would maintain that it all comes down to being serious about caring and truth-seeking. As the pioneering educator Madeline Hunter once famously put it, "Students don't care how much you know until they know how much you care." While pandering to lowered standards may make many college teachers and administrators feel better about themselves, this really doesn't embody genuine concern for nontraditional students. Is a watered-down college education really a service to those who've been—and still are being—systematically belittled and excluded? Are we college planners and teachers going to foist a *redoubled* compact of complacency on groups and individuals who have already been handed the short straw? And, for that matter, are such people really so obtuse as to not notice when ham-handed spoon-feeding replaces high expectations and first-rate instruction?

Might genuine regard for disadvantaged populations require us instead to figure out how to provide everybody with the real lightning in the bottle that truly great college experiences can provide? I am convinced that genuine regard would require both more attention to non-privileged needs *and* a commitment to harder and better work as teachers and students. Non-elite students aren't stupid, and we ought not to backhandedly suggest that they somehow are. We ought, instead, to help them lay hands on the intellectual skills and treasures that non-complacent versions of college can offer.

In this chapter, I relay some of my thoughts on how we might really, truly serve those students who most need more and better from us.

The Importance of Teaching Styles

Standard lectures do no students any favor, but I suspect the performance gap (between black and white students, for example) is larger for courses taught that way, which means they present an equity problem in addition to their other problems. If you reflect on this, you'll eventually come to this question: Why would anyone deliberately rely so heavily on a method that increases the burden on black students, first-generation college students, and so on? Don't they have enough burdens already? Perhaps they feel ill at ease. Many nontraditional students haven't gone through the pre-socialization to college that their more advantaged peers have gone through in the kinds of high schools that graduate most seniors to higher education. Some students already feel they do not belong (and some traditional students and others will make comments asserting that they don't). These students already have more pressures from home, including financial pressures.

While colleges may offer a full ride to poor students, those students often have to help out at home to deal with a crisis such as a health problem, divorce, or eviction. Certainly, all students' time at college can be derailed by such a catastrophe, but the razor's edge that poor students ride and the pressures that come with that are obvious. As their teacher, you can help to mitigate this by telling these students you are happy they are at your college. They don't all know that. And not everyone conveys that message, either implicitly or explicitly.

Diversity in the Classroom

Your department is composed of experts in different areas of your subject. No history department is full of scholars who focus solely on Latin American history. No English department is all poets. No engineering faculty is only mechanical engineers. That variety gives your department a more comprehensive relationship to your field. The same holds true for diversity in terms of race, gender, age, nationality, and other traits. Hopefully, your department is also diverse in those ways, and hopefully your classroom is too!

While you don't really have any say about which students enroll in your classes, you must make an effort to recruit TAs who are not obviously the same as you. Diverse TAs show *all* your undergraduates that you don't have to be whatever the professor is (old, tall, white, male, etc.) to go into and succeed within your field. Research also shows that students of color do better when their TA is a member of their racial group.[1] Specifically, researchers found that, for several reasons, "students received better grades in classes taken with TAs who were of a similar race." Students, for example, seem to be "more likely to attend their TAs' optional discussion sections and office hours when the TA was of a similar race." (This result also implies that *all* students are more engaged and do better work when they meet with TAs in extra sessions and office hours, so you can ask your TAs to hold such sessions as part of their job, suggesting ways to ensure that students come.)

Diversifying your TA crew might require some unconventional moves. At the University of Vermont, professors in sociology recruited junior and senior majors as TAs for large classes, since we had no graduate students. They performed at least as well as grad students, perhaps because they were not simultaneously worried about finishing their theses or dissertations. It was sometimes hard to find TAs of color, but since I was teaching "Race Relations," it did not seem competent to me to recruit only white students. Hence I conducted a wide talent search, including students who were not sociology majors.

Professors also need to mentor students, especially those who *need* it. According to a 2018 report by Audrey Williams June, significant disparity exists in this crucial component of the college experience. "Professors," June relates, "dominate the role of undergraduate mentor," with "nearly two-thirds of alumni who had a mentor during college [saying] that person was a professor." Yet, when surveyed, "just 47 percent of alumni of color said they'd had a mentor on the faculty, compared with 72 percent of white graduates."[2] This is systematic and meaningful discriminatory treatment, and it is within the power of every college teacher to be aware of it and combat it.

Racial diversity is not the only priority you ought to address when recruiting TAs. Another important form of diversity is age. Older students typically have more learning and experiences than their younger classmates. They can often more readily see how new concepts integrate with their prior knowledge, and they may be more likely to ask to see practical applications for what you are teaching.

However, as you engage with your students and ask for their insights and understandings about your subject, never use one student to stand for a group. There is no "Black viewpoint," "Muslim viewpoint," "Japanese viewpoint." To ask someone to speak for a group, religion, or nation implies that such collectivities are monolithic. It also puts extra pressure on an individual who may already feel burdened simply by the task of speaking in class.

Battling Gender And Other Stereotypes

The most common form of diversity is, of course, gender. We all regularly encounter people of another gender. Nevertheless, teachers do not always treat male and female students equally.

Perhaps the evidence of this problem is most commonly found in

STEM courses. Everyone "knows" that girls are worse than boys in math and science. (Just ask former Harvard president and influential political consultant Lawrence H. Summers, who, in 2005, infamously attributed women's underrepresentation in math and science to "issues of intrinsic aptitude.") While there is still a gender participation gap in many STEM fields, this arises from girls being treated differently than boys in high school with respect to the hard sciences. Although the "intrinsic aptitude" bias persists, the performance gap is happily shrinking. Studies show that girls in environments with more women in STEM professions are more likely to take STEM classes and that girls are performing as well as boys in high school math assessments.

It's a very human attitude for an individual to assume that she is essentially a good person. And of course, we know that "good people aren't biased." *But!* Don't assume that you have no bias. As college teachers, we cannot rely on our prejudices to understand our students. We have to figure out how to deliver the actual goods to all of our students rather than perpetuating stereotypical, if often well-meaning, cultural tropes, and inadvertently driving certain groups of students from our classes and subjects. Assess your own expectations of your students. Are you teaching all of them? Do you subtly expect more from some students than from others? Do you call on some more than others? Make more eye contact? Give them more reinforcements (subtle or not) after their answers?

Project Implicit at Harvard University offers free online tests that help reveal how we have been socialized to view people from racial backgrounds that are different from our own.[3] Results from these tests could be useful to faculty members, as they may reveal deeply held assumptions that play out in embarrassing, destructive, and sometimes hurtful ways in college classrooms. Reflect on these behaviors and how you can resist them.

I've already pointed out that very few professors have enrolled in pedagogy classes or taken education courses. Clearly, then, most professors have never been in a classroom that discussed the literature about diverse students. Most have never read the literature about teacher expectations. Consequently, few have had the opportunity to reflect on these matters, especially to think in groups or with the help of a professor or reading material. This inexperience leads to professors repeating the patterns they experienced as students. This is what so many people do in so many other arenas, too!

In our classes, more and more evidence shows us that these old instructional methods are not the most effective, especially not for many types of students. Just as doctors are expected to stay on top of changes in treatments or surgeries, we should expect professors to maintain, as part of their ethos, best practices with regard to diversity issues in their pedagogy. And it's important to have that training, because people are generally not aware of their implicit biases.

But neither should you explicitly confess your biases. "While it may feel empowering to reveal your bias in public," advises rhetoric expert Kathleen Tarr, "be aware that some people still believe any admission of bias is an admission of guilty behavior. To be so transparent is an individual choice, and not a decision you should take lightly."[4] People will take it wrong. Some will not realize that it's an act of humility to admit bias. They may even take it as a warning, and thus conclude that they should be on the lookout that you will be biased against *them*. Other people will recognize that admitting bias is an important part of the "standard" race relations workshop, so it marks you as a "good" person. But still other folks may make a very different conclusion: He's not only biased, he's so biased he thinks it's okay to talk about it in public!

In class, when appropriate and relevant, you can open up about yourself, your own life, and hopefully students will feel it's okay to open up about theirs. You can be rueful about decisions or opportunities lost. Tell them some things about yourself, your own life, but refrain from sharing information about your religion and perhaps your politics. As illustration, at one point I lost some members of my audience by making fun of George H.W. Bush when I could just as well have chosen John F. Kennedy for an example. Keep 'em guessing. You can think of yourself as an assortment of different bumper stickers. Oftentimes, if you see one bumper sticker on a car, you can guess the rest. Don't let your students know you as a predictable set of bumper stickers.

At many schools, professors are likely to lose their right-wing students, because most professors live in a left-wing environment, so we forget that the world is not like us. You do not want to lose anyone! I had a colleague at UVM who actively *did* want to lose her anti-feminist students, especially if they were male. Some race relations teachers *do* want to lose their racist students. But these are just the students we should be trying to reach, not lose!

Moreover, they have something to teach us. At the very least, they teach us ways of thinking about "the other side." Surely they teach us, as well, that people on "the other side" can be funny, intelligent, can love, can hold reasonable positions on many other matters. Beyond this, they can teach us the kernel of truth that often lies within what may seem to us a benighted worldview. There is no real growth in preaching to a choir that echoes your ideas; finding new and innovative ways to engage students is one of the joys of pedagogy, and what student would you more like to bring into an engaging discussion than a skeptic?

Students with Disabilities

Even when a student's disability, mental or physical, may be obvious, some professors betray a pent-up frustration about accommodating a student if they seek any kind of exemption from the normal requirements of a course. Such teachers seem to feel as though they are putting their finger in the dike to hold back the flood: If they fail to uphold the requirement to the letter, Western civilization may perish. Or they may feel that these students are doing their best to skate by, doing as little work as possible while benefiting from their accommodations.

But students with learning accommodations for their disabilities are almost never trying to "game the system." They are trying to survive a learning environment not designed for them, which is why accommodations are mandatory under the Americans with Disabilities Act. Usually, you can meet these students' needs while maintaining the integrity of your course and its grading system. If a professor is worrying about the dike collapsing, it usually means they are overemphasizing the certification function of a course. If you can approach a student who asks for extra time, an audio version of the text, or some other accommodation as someone who is trying to maximize their learning, you will be teaching that student just as you want to teach *all* students.

Sharing Resources

One of the easiest ways to reinforce the content of your course to your students is to make it available to them in multiple venues. Begin class by going over the skeletal outline of the lesson and put it on the whiteboard or chalkboard. An outline will allow them to understand the path forward for the lesson and see connections to material already covered. Meanwhile, if you share your lecture notes with them on whatever digital platform your institution uses, they can refer to it whenever they feel lost—there's no reason not to! Put your Power-Point slides up on the platform. If you quote someone, put the quote up. If you show a video, post it so students can see it again. If you are reluctant to do any of this, perhaps it stems from a lingering worry about spoon-feeding your students the answer, but the goal is to help the students learn the material so that it sticks, rather than to hope they read your mind, take comprehensive notes the first time you say something, or feel so lost they look for breadcrumbs elsewhere.

Some of the accommodations you develop for students with learn-ing disabilities may actually help all students. Consider the curb cut—the ramp at a street corner or crosswalk built for people in wheelchairs. Don't they help you too? Every time I walk to the Metro here in Washington, DC, en route to the airport or train station, I pull my carry-on bag down and up those ramps and am relieved that people with disabilities inspired their installation. So are parents with strollers, neighbors with shopping carts—everyone, really, at some point in our lives.[5]

So, consider the benefit of curb-cut equivalents in teaching and learning. For example, Katie Linder has shown that providing closed captions and transcripts for visuals used in lectures enhances learning for all students.[6] All of us have at some point struggled to read Pow-erPoint slides with small print from the back of the room. Providing a printout of the most important and densest slides helps everyone, as does access to copies of the lecture notes. The students whose indi-vidual needs prompt you to clarify your slides or provide a transcript do a service to all your students by providing an opportunity for more thoughtful pedagogy. I have also found that giving extra time for an in-class exam leads to better answers for some students and also prompts me to construct better questions.[7]

Just as we all have implicit biases for and against certain groups, so, too, do we have behaviors that communicate those biases. The process of constructing accommodations for students with special needs will help you to acknowledge the existence of biases and behaviors in your teaching you weren't even aware of.

The Importance of High Expectations

When my son became a high school English teacher, my first and most important piece of advice to him was to have high expectations of all his students. Make a practice of telling your students, "You *will* do good work in this course!" and anticipate that they will. Saying this lets them know that is what you expect and that you will help them to work toward a high standard of achievement. Ask students on the first day of class if they are willing to meet the class's expectations. Are they willing to be on time? To prepare? To participate intellectually? If they are, they will be much closer to the success they seek. When you call on students you should do so expecting them to know the answer. Don't rely on your biased impressions of student types. Jocks can have great answers! Nontraditional students can blow you away with their lived knowledge. I had the good fortune to begin my teaching career at a historically Black college of considerable merit. Some of the students there were better than my best students at the University of Vermont, who were almost uniformly white and more advantaged.

Your students are diverse in lots of ways. Avoid categorizing them. In the abstract, I found my UVM students to be overprivileged, under-thoughtful children of the rich. Thinking this did not help me reach them or teach them. If you avoid categorizing them, you will avoid stereotyping them. And in terms of individual students, you must avoid writing off any student, for whatever reason, whether it be for their politics, attitude, demeanor, or past behavior. Always respect and embody academic freedom. This will allow your students the freedom to hold their convictions while also requiring them to have support and rationale for them, as well as challenging them to reflect on their own beliefs and biases. *All* students need a respectful environment in which all individuals and almost all ideas are valid and valued.

Never accept a student's assessment that they are "bad" at some aspect of your course. "Until now," you have to tell them, "you've been bad at statistics." There is a completely different feel to, "Until now, foreign languages have not been your forte," or "Until now, you've not been a good writer." Your high expectations mean that their negative assessment is no longer going to hold true. This is not a panacea, however; you still have to teach them the skills they lack, and both you and the student will need to put in the work to master the course's content. But expecting them to do well creates a sense of obligation in your student as well as an understanding of the quality of work required.

If a student is giving off signals *not* to call on him, discuss that with him in private. Ask him to see you in your office. Some people prefer to process information and ideas internally before offering input, certainly. Ask him if that's the case. If it isn't, describe to him as specifically as you can how he is signaling to you that you should not to expect much from him. Ask: "Was that your purpose?" As well, point out that other students almost certainly have the same sorts of questions he does, and his asking the questions helps both him and others. Strategize about how to get past this and explain why that matters. One technique is for the both of you to devise a subtle signal he can give that communicates he needs time to prepare a response before you call on him.

Students from less privileged backgrounds often do not know how good they already are. I once told a student at UVM that she was a top participant in my seminar. She had no idea, and didn't think of herself as good at all, but I was able to show her the data I kept on class participation. Similarly, at Tougaloo, I once taught a psychology major who learned chi-square statistical analysis on her own, but thought she was not good enough to apply for Vanderbilt, owing to her nonstellar SAT scores.

You should be aware of impostor syndrome, in which some students, often due to their class, race, gender, sexuality, or special needs, feel that their presence at the university is somehow illegitimate. Such individuals may think and fear that they "do not belong here" and that it's only a matter of time before their lack of ability is exposed.

In a phenomenon known as "stereotype threat," minority students are especially likely to doubt their ability; the social psychologist Claude Steele found in studies that just telling Black students they are taking a standardized test to rate their ability led his target group to do worse. When another group of Black students taking the same test were told beforehand that the test was unimportant, they did better. Students from the working class may doubt their ability too, questioning their right to be in college.

We need to bridge this chasm, which is often not as wide as we presume. As counterintuitive as it may seem, being direct and clear about your high expectations is key. If students aren't meeting your expectations, you must let them know. When five or six of my Tougaloo students did not do well in Methods and Statistics of Social Research, I made them take a makeup in the January term. Likewise, at UVM, when one Urban Sociology class was really flailing on the material, I postponed the next unit and had them take another shot at learning the bobbled material. Actively correcting them and reminding them that I expected better effectively communicated what they needed to do, and that doing less was not acceptable.

Northwestern University has taken a systematic approach to investigating the importance of high expectations. It has placed half of struggling biology students who volunteered to be eligible for extra help into an honors seminar that meets in addition to the regular class, to discuss major issues in the field. These students, regardless of race, generally do better back in the underlying biology course than those volunteers left out of the honors-level meetings. Yet black students had done *worse* than white students in the regular, lower-expectations course.[8] The power of high expectations is quite extraordinary.[9]

The lesson is clear: Don't let yourself develop poor expectations for *any* student, even those who have poor expectations of themselves. Expect them to hand their work in on time. Point out that there are built-in reasons for this, not just that it's a requirement. (For instance, first drafts of a paper will get shared with another student for comment, and that student must have the paper to do so!) I also explain that enforcing deadlines for assignments helps to protect the student from being overwhelmed by a buildup of work as the semester progresses.

Expectations are *especially* important in remedial courses, where many students expect to fail. Most affluent white students, especially if they went to prep schools, will feel empowered to come to your office hours or make an appointment to see you. They may not always do it, but most of them feel they can. Other students may know this, too, but only in an abstract sense. First-generation college students might not quite understand what office hours are for or be intimidated to make use of them.[10] Partly for that reason, early in the course, require that every student see you in your office for ten minutes if you have fewer than, say, forty students. This requirement should be structured into your course outline. Of course, you need a reason for the requirement. Here are three:

—To discuss their idea for a term paper or research project, if your course includes such an assignment

—To give back the first exam and talk about it

—To tell you how they see your course being relevant to their major or their future job

Tell them that you will also ask them, "What question or comment do you have about the course that you have not asked or expressed in class?" If you think that their question or comment should be voiced in the class, tell the student to do so next time. This gets them talking in class. If it's a more idiosyncratic question, then discuss it in your office. But the main point is that requiring a first visit may get them more comfortable reaching out to you for help.

My conclusion is that issues of equity and inclusion are rightly and squarely on our agenda now, but that the same challenge applies to our work in this dimension as in the overall task of college teaching: We must do better. To do that, we must confront *both* the old complicity that kept colleges from fully (or even partially) recognizing the ways in which they perpetuated established group privileges *and* the new complacency that implies developing and maintaining high achievement standards is somehow a part of the old regime. It is not. Our challenge, after all, is to deliver a higher education to anybody and everybody, rather than to just the traditional, comfortable few.

In the end, of course, you are designing the class you teach. So much is up to you! Our students are trusting us to help them learn, and that's the core of the job. If we decide, either explicitly or implicitly, that we will teach only part of the population of our class, we have done a disservice to not just the students, but their families and communities. Helping students who are isolated, either socially or academically, privately or publicly, will make you and your classes better and more educative. And I'm stridently telling you: Own your course! Expect great things from your students. Be shocked when they don't meet those expectations! Don't hold yourself aloof from your students, remaining blase about their miseducation or lack of education. Teaching our students well is the bedrock of our society, and letting students skate by or allowing them to leave our class confused or ignorant means we are sending students out into their adulthood without tools and skills to help all people as we wrestle with the problems, old and new, in our world.

11

Ending Well

In this last chapter, I offer some thoughts both on how to conclude your individual courses, and on what larger conclusions you might bear in mind as you keep refining your craft as a college teacher.

As you teach, you will learn to recognize what choices work well in your classroom and what you might improve on to help your students be successful. I've given examples in this book of instances where I realized that I needed to change my practice to be a better educator. And your students are a terrific source of advice, too, although many professors might doubt that. Most schools now rely on student evaluations of professors and classes as their source of feedback. In addition to those surveys, if you hand out your own custom course evaluations, do so at the start of the last class, not toward the end. Otherwise, students won't write much—they'll simply leave. Also ask your students to write a letter of advice to students taking this course next year, providing a list of possible items to cover:

—Things to watch out for
—What's easy, what's hard
—Hints on how to deal with the readings

—What do you wish you had known about the course when
you started?

—What do you wish you had done differently?

In addition to having the students complete the college's pro forma
evaluation, you might also invite them to hand in written answers to
either of these questions:

—If I had this course to do over again, I would avoid my biggest mistake, which was _____.

—My best advice for people taking this course next year is

_____.

Or you could accomplish the same thing in an oral format, by having students pair up and ask each other, "What will you carry from
this course?" If the answer is "nothing," the alternative question is,
"What did you hope to carry from this course?" Then, invite pairs to
volunteer to answer the second question. After a few have, call on one
or two more and ask them which question they'd rather answer and
let them answer it.

You might ask them, "Before I took this course, I thought
_____ ["sociology" or "Walt Whitman" or . . .] was
_____. Now I think it is _____."

Finally, you may want to set up a tradition of a special last
class—perhaps include a visitor or maybe hold an "unconference,"
a loosely structured event at which students present their projects
through some visual means—a poster or web page, perhaps. The
point is to figure out a fun and educational way to make this last class
session a useful review and learning experience.

A possible related assignment: Ask students to review the syllabus and write a paragraph on the piece of writing, video, or other work that meant the most to them, that they will remember long after the course is over. Discuss their choices in class; this will get students thinking about how the course endures in their minds You could also invite them to write a paragraph about the piece of writing, video, or other work that they think you should drop, explaining why. This triggers students to review the course and is helpful revision for you as the instructor.

If your class is a prerequisite for a follow-up seminar, the last assignment might ask the student to describe the proposed research or project that they will do in the seminar. You might also challenge prospective follow-up students in a final session to do something that certifies they have qualified for such a course. This could give that next course a cachet: Its enrollees are the elect! It also would show students not intending to take the subsequent seminar the value of what they have learned.

Avoid the kind of closure that implies, "Now you have learned sociology (or American history, or biology, or whatever)." Instead, ask:

—"What will you remember from this course five years hence?"
—"What will you use from this course in your professional life?"
—"Have you talked with your parents/roommate/best friend about any ideas from this course? If so, what did they make of it?"

Have students write down their answers as their final journal entries before the last class, then discuss as a class.

Your Own Ending

Course endings are also unique moments for you, the teacher. Developing good wrap-up habits can pay great future dividends. You should devote a whole day to the process and keep pondering ways to refine it. Here, I offer a few suggestions.

Immediately after the last day of class, rethink your course and write down notes about how you will change it next time you teach it. Better yet, if you've been keeping notes throughout the semester on how things have gone, review and incorporate those.

Leave all the stuff from your course up on the web. Tell students it will be there, should they want to refer to it. Why? Because somewhere, someday, they will think about something you taught them and may want to excavate it for themselves or someone else.

Many years ago, I read this paragraph from James Agee's *Let Us Now Praise Famous Men*, his amazing study of three white sharecropper families in the Great Depression:

> How did we get caught? Why is it things always seem to go against us? Why is it there can't ever be any pleasure in living? I'm so tired it don't seem like I ever could get rest enough. I'm as tired when I get up in the morning as I am when I lay down at night. Sometimes it seems like there wouldn't never be no end to it, nor even a let-up. One year it'll look like things was going to be pretty good; but you get a little bit of money saved, something always happens.

I love that paragraph, and I want to reflect on it from time to time, so I keep it in my active files. Sadly, I also sometimes yearn for a long paragraph that a student at Tougaloo College, decades ago, wrote in response to my exam question on socialization, in which she explained better than Freud ever did how we internalize ideas into the superego. Alas, because I hadn't yet learned the importance of saving important things for posterity, I failed to save that student's classic phrasing.

Hopefully, some student someday will want to access some part of the material you put online for your course. Maybe it will even be an exam question, or the inspirational quotation with which you led off the second unit.

"I stop somewhere, waiting for you," Walt Whitman wrote. Who knows where or why your students will again pause to reflect on something of importance to them in your course? And if you are certain that such a moment of looking back on the course will never happen, then why teach it? If, on the other hand, you do think what you teach is important, then tell your students you will leave the material on the web for them. Doing so implies to them that what they learned is important and worth reflecting back on in the future.

The Larger Meaning of College

One of my core beliefs is that the United States needs engaged and knowledgeable citizens to make our country a better place. I also think this sacred process of teaching has a necessary anchor in the truth. Truth has always been at the core of my efforts, both as a researcher and teacher. Truth-seeking matters, in both directions: Just as telling the truth about the past helps foster justice in the present, achieving justice in the present helps us to tell the truth about the past. When I heard my students' flawed understanding of Reconstruction at Tougaloo, I realized that miseducation is a weapon of oppression. That's why I wrote a state textbook for Mississippi called *Mississippi: Conflict and Change*, because Black students in the state were kept in positions of inferiority in part through their poor education. I hope you have a similar belief about the value of education and that you put it into practice so that your students leave your class better educated and, therefore, better citizens in service of others.

The great idea is, of course, to keep expanding this process. This is more complicated than it sounds, and college is where people—both students and their instructors—get to ponder deeply (and begin to savor) the things that help us all see and think anew. My hope is that this small book will nourish ideas and techniques that you and other disciplined truth-seekers will deploy when and where it really matters, which, in our hurried commercial society, is still largely the precious and concentrated time that young people spend inside institutions of higher education.

I will close with a story from my earliest years of teaching, which perhaps speaks to my overall message.

During the summer of 1965, while a graduate student, I ran the "Social Science Lab" at Tougaloo College, which is in Madison County, near Jackson, Mississippi.[1] On August 25, the Johnson administration sent federal voting registrars to several counties in Mississippi that had proven particularly reluctant to register African Americans to vote. The next day, curious to see the scene for myself, I drove to the town of Canton, the county seat of Madison County. There, the registrars had rented a vacant storefront on the courthouse square.

A card table with a folding chair, on which sat a white registrar, were the only furnishings inside the otherwise bare room. From this table, in a line that stretched to the door, African Americans waited calmly to register. Outside, the line doubled in number and stretched east to the end of the block, where it turned south, ran another block, reached the corner, turned west, and reached the end of that block. The wait time was more than a day, until the Department of Justice added two more card tables and two more registrars.

Those waiting seemed not to mind. Some had been waiting for decades to register to vote; another day wouldn't exhaust their patience. A spirit of jubilee—not boisterous, just quiet satisfaction—floated in the air. Everyone in line knew that the Democrats, at that time the party of white supremacy, had for decades made it extremely difficult if not outright impossible for African Americans to vote in Mississippi and especially in Madison County. Now it was their turn. That scene—of hopeful masses yearning for democracy—made a lifelong impression on me.

For years since Reconstruction, Southern Democrats had simply prevaricated about the capacity of African American citizens to vote responsibly. For example, a 1921 article in the magazine *Confederate Veteran* asserted that, during Reconstruction, widespread fraud prevailed among Black voters, encouraged by white Republicans: "Armed troops were kept at every county seat to uphold negro rule and encourage him to vote the Republican ticket as often as he pleased, the Republicans by this means running up great majorities." Newly freed African Americans certainly voted in massive numbers across the South during Reconstruction. But though many were illiterate, they voted their interests with great responsibility. Across the South, they oversaw the adoption of the most democratic state constitutions that the Southern states have ever had, far better in fact than the constitutions under which they operate today.

It's hard not to notice that today's suppression of truth is part of a new assault on the hard-won breakthroughs I recall from 1965. Today, the Republican Party, not the Democrats, have become the party of white supremacy, and modern-day Republicans seem set on doing what they can to keep Black (and poor and transient and Latino) voters from voting, including by again alleging fraud in heavily Black districts.[2] Now, as in Reconstruction, such allegations are simply not true. But the stratagem of lying and counting on the citizenry's passive acceptance of voter suppression is as old as it is crude and dangerous.

I mention this continuing conflict at the end of this book because it underscores the importance not just of seeking the truth, but of transmitting to students a hunger for doing so. Here, I tend to get into trouble with a certain strain of thinking that asks: "Why should we privilege one account above others?" We now have all kinds of academicians (and politicians!) talking about the possibility of alternative truths and implying that such crude relativism may be more useful and appropriate for us in the present.

The problem with this fashionable stance is that it discounts terms like "true" and "false." Yet despite all its complexities and injustices, a great deal of history actually rests on bedrock of fact. I remain convinced that, no matter what discipline you teach, showing your students how your field of inquiry relates to the overarching project of building a more truthful and just world is one of the great advantages of genuinely cutting-edge college teaching. If you equip people to perceive and pursue this ultimate lodestar, you will, I am sure, keep yourself—and thus all of us—moving forward toward a better society.

Editor's Note

My father left the classroom years before the Hydra-headed challenge of students using artificial intelligence content generation programs reared its many heads, so he did not address it in his manuscript. As educators nowadays know, nearly everyone is trying to figure out how to use AI as a useful pedagogical tool as well as how to thwart students from using AI to game the system.

I am not so naive as to think my dad would have some silver bullet to solve this difficult and perplexing issue, but I think that many of his ideas in this book are quite helpful in addressing the less intellectual applications of AI. For example, stressing to students the idea of the "supportive critiquing community" suggests that their ideas and reactions are more important to their peers and to you when they are genuine and thoughtful. The inspiring message of the famous Teddy Roosevelt quote my father uses early in this book ("Far and away the best prize that life has to offer is the chance to work hard at work worth doing") might move students to reflect on what they lose when they retreat to submitting something they haven't come up with.

And if neither of those strategies works, in later chapters, there are ideas and suggestions for how to create assessments that are more meaningful for students, thus leading to their understanding that this is their idea, their work, and they should value that work and those ideas. Too often, the focus of school for these students is on valuing the completion of an assignment. Working with students and seeing their drafts, conferencing with them about their writing, and helping them improve will aid them in their learning and in valuing the work, in their subsequent college classes and afterward. It will also create an impediment to turning in a one-off AI piece that perhaps sounds impressive but actually contains no original thought or understanding.

Finally, his idea of an oral final exam is another way to negate the influence of AI content generation. Using this type of creative thinking and this novel approach to assessments can both help students to better learn and understand the material and concepts you are teaching and discourage students from using material that isn't their own work. Of course, as some of his anecdotes illustrate, like the one about a Ladysmith Black Mambazo concert, some students are not going to buy what you're selling. But some of the ideas and techniques in the book may help you to mitigate the problem of artificially generated work being passed off as a student's original thinking.

—Nicholas Loewen

Acknowledgments

I would like to acknowledge Lucy Loewen McMurrer, Mary Loewen Cavalier, and Susan Loewen for all their help in trying to piece together anecdotes and memories from the manuscript, as well as their sage advice in their reading and suggesting revisions to the draft. I would also like to acknowledge Jeniva Miller for her thoughtful, careful, and insightful suggestions and ideas. I would like to thank Michael Dawson for taking on this project and for allowing me to lean on his writing and teaching experiences. Above all, I'd like to thank Dad for entrusting Michael and me with the manuscript and for being a terrific teacher and even better father.

—*Nicholas Loewen*

I thank Nick Loewen and Lucy Loewen McMurrer for including me in this gratifying and important project. I thank my life partner, Kathleen Gardipee, for her constant interest in and encouragement of my work with Jim and Nick. I especially thank Nick for his enthusiasm, diligence, and skill. Your dad's spirit is alive and well in you.

—*Michael Dawson*

Notes

Introduction

1. Richard Arum and Josipa Roksa, *Academically Adrift: Limited Learning on College Campuses* (Chicago: University of Chicago Press, 2011), 4–8. According to the authors' broad survey of U.S. college students, 50 percent of sophomores did not take a single course all year that required a total of twenty pages of writing. Thirty-three percent of sophomores did not take a single course that required more than forty pages of reading each week.

2. Since it's my field, let me supply here a thumbnail introduction to the sociology of knowledge. Paraphrasing Karl Mannheim, people, strictly speaking, do not think. Rather, they think further what others have thought before. We all inherit a culture with patterns of thought that we deem appropriate to a given situation. To understand our thinking, we need to examine its social and cultural origins, not just our own mind. See Karl Mannheim, *Ideology and Utopia* (New York: Harcourt, Brace, & World, 1968 [1936]), 2–3.

3. Arum and Roksa, *Academically Adrift*, 121.

4. I know various professors who, when their campuses got shut down by the occasional student strike, told me they welcomed the break, because they could get more of "their work" done. I believe such faculty members are an affront to the profession and a detriment to their department and school, even if they do bring in grants and make a difference within their discipline. At worst, they misuse tuition monies to support their private research. Admittedly, you may not share that harsh opinion; and you need not share it in order to make use of this book. What matters most is that you care about teaching and see it as part of "your work."

5. Roger Martin, "Let's Focus More on the First Year," *Inside Higher Education*, February 29, 2016, insidehighered.com/views/2016/02/29/we-must-pay-more-attention-first-year-college-essay.

6. Harvard does now have the Derek Bok Center for Teaching and Learning, but it seems directed more toward current Harvard faculty than to graduate students. To be sure, it does offer support to current Harvard TAs, who are graduate students, and does represent a major advance over the lack of such support when I was there.

7. Stacey Patton, "Student Evaluations: Feared, Loathed, and Not Going Anywhere," *Chronicle of Higher Education*, May 19, 2015, chroniclevitae.com/news/1011-student-evaluations-feared-loathed-and-not-going-anywhere; Vimal Patel, "Training Graduate Students to Be Effective Teachers," *Chronicle of Higher Education*, July 30, 2017, chronicle.com/article/Training-Graduate-Students-to/240783. Also in the *Chronicle*, Leonard Cassuto called universities' commitment to training graduates as teachers "tissue-thin." ("What If They Fail Teacher Training?" February 26, 2017, chronicle.com/article/What-if-They-Fail-Teacher/239310). Arum and Roksa, *Academically Adrift*, 6, 133.

8. Stuart L. Hart, "The Third-Generation Corporation," in *The Oxford Handbook of Business and the Environment*, ed. Pratima Bansal and Andrew J. Hoffman (New York: Oxford University Press, 2012), 648–55; Laurie Bassi, Ed Frauenheim, and Dan McMurrer, *Good Company: Business Success in the Worthiness Era* (San Francisco: Berrett-Koehler, 2011).

9. Talking with professors, I find many who recall every moment of mentoring they experienced—often all too few of them—but engage in even less mentoring themselves.

10. Studies show that students who take intro courses from adjuncts are less likely to continue or graduate in a field. Beckie Supiano, "It Matters a Lot Who Teaches Introductory Courses. Here's Why," *Chronicle of Higher Education*, April 15, 2018, chronicle.com/article/It-Matters-a-Lot-Who-Teaches/243125.

11. The website Tomorrow Professor (tomprof.stanford.edu), now deactivated, suggested some reasons why new instructors, particularly, overprepare:

- You love teaching (you find course prep and classroom interaction more stimulating than research).

- You mistakenly equate "great teaching" with delivering enormous amounts of content in each class period.

- You feel insecure about your job performance. You are highly sensitive to students' evaluations of your teaching.

- You believe it's somehow possible to please everyone so if you spend more time, you will teach better and receive unanimously positive evaluations.

- You feel you have to be twice as good to be judged as equal. You have unrealistically high expectations about teaching. You often feel like a fraud or impostor, so over-preparing for your classes protects you from being discovered.

- You have a profound fear of failure in the areas of research and publication (teaching becomes a form of procrastination from writing). You have never thought about how you're spending your time and have unconsciously fallen into the teaching trap because of the built-in accountability that standing in front of a classroom full of students several times a week provides.

- Your professors were poor teachers when you were in college and you're trying to be different and better for your students (i.e., the professor you never had).

- If you're an underrepresented faculty member, the dynamics of racism and sexism in the classroom mean that you don't get the benefit of the doubt from students, so you over-prepare in order to prove you deserve to be teaching in a college classroom.

12. Arum and Roksa cite data showing that faculty members on average spend just eleven hours per week in class, preparing for class, grading, advising, and otherwise meeting with students. On the other hand, they spend just five hours per week doing research if they are at a large research-oriented institution and just two hours per week if at a liberal arts college. See *Academically Adrift* (Chicago: University of Chicago Press, 2011), 8. Where does the time go? We all know, of course: emails, meetings, reviewing manuscripts, and doing other things connected to one's field.

13. James W. Loewen died after a two-year battle with cancer, on August 19, 2021.

14. Helen Sword, *Stylish Academic Writing* (Cambridge, MA: Harvard University Press, 2012), 23.

15. Sword, *Stylish Academic Writing*, 23–24.

1. Designing Your Course

1. C. Wright Mills, *The Sociological Imagination* (NewYork: Oxford University Press, 1959), 3.

2. Donna Killian Duffy and Janet Wright Jones, *Teaching Within the Rhythms of the Semester* (Hoboken, NJ: John Wiley & Sons, 1995).

3. The advent of AI technology has made plagiarism easier, See Editor's Note at the end of this volume.

2. The First Day of Class

1. If you don't have a website or don't know how to use it, leave the video with your department's administrative assistant on a flash drive or ask that the department post it on its website.

2. Ken Bain, *What the Best College Teachers Do* (Cambridge, MA: Harvard University Press, 2004), 18.

3. Elizabeth F. Barkley, *Student Engagement Techniques: A Handbook for College Faculty* (San Francisco: Jossey-Bass Wiley, 2010), 12, citing Jonathan Brown and Bernard Weiner, "Affective Consequences of Ability Versus Effort Ascriptions," *Journal of Educational Psychology* 76, no. 1 (1984): 146–58.

4. "Professors Share: The Moment that Changed the Way I Teach," *Chronicle of Higher Education*, December 5, 2018, https://chronicle.com/article/professors-share-the-moment-that-changed-the-way-i-teach/?sra=true.

5. Barbara Jones, former director of the American Library Association's Office for Intellectual Freedom and executive director of the Freedom to Read Foundation, quoted in Colleen Flaherty, "Trigger Warnings Ahead," *Inside Higher Education*, July 20, 2017, insidehighered.com/news/2017/07/20/new-book-seeks-round-out-trigger-warning-debate-competing-histories-case-studies.

6. Tennessee Code 49-6-1019(a)(6).

7. Committee A on Academic Freedom and Tenure, "On Trigger Warnings," American Association of University Professors, August 2014, https://www.aaup.org/report/trigger-warnings.

8. Oberlin College, Office of Equity Concerns, "Support Resources for Faculty," available at https://web.archive.org/web/20131222174936/http:/new.oberlin.edu/office/equity-concerns/sexual-offense-resource-guide/prevention-support-education/support-resources-for-faculty.dot.

3. The Importance of Writing

1. Colleen Flaherty, "When More Is Less," *Inside Higher Ed*, December 3, 2015, https://www.insidehighered.com/news/2015/12/04/writing-study-finds-quality-assignment-and-instruction-not-quantity-matters.

2. Sarah Rose Cavanagh, *The Spark of Learning: Energizing the College Classroom with the Science of Emotion* (Morgantown: West Virginia University Press, 2016), 145.

3. Derek Bok, *Our Underachieving Colleges: A Candid Look at How Much Students Learn and Why They Should Be Learning More*, rev. ed. (Princeton, NJ: Princeton University Press, 2007).

4. See Rick Reis, "Do Your Students Really Understand You Assignments?" available at https://web.archive.org/web/20151230165533/cgi.stanford.edu/~dept-ctl/tomprof/posting.php?ID=857.

5. Ken Bain, *What the Best College Teachers Do* (Cambridge, MA: Harvard University Press, 2004), 18.

6. Angela Baldasare, Melissa Vito, and Vincent J. Del Casino Jr., "When a B Isn't Good Enough," *Inside Higher Ed*, November 14, 2016, https://www.insidehighered.com/views/2016/11/15/developing-metrics-and-models-are-vital-student-learning-and-retention-essay.

7. Rob Jenkins, "Why I Don't Edit Their Rough Drafts," *Chronicle of Higher Education*, December 11, 2016, chronicle.com/article/Why-I-Don-t-Edit-Their-Rough/238618.

8. Erick Sierra, "How a Google Spreadsheet Saved My Literature Class," *Chronicle of Higher Education*, April 10, 2016, https://www.chronicle.com/article/how-a-google-spreadsheet-saved-my-literature-class/.

9. Sam Wineburg and Sarah McGrew, "Why Students Can't Google Their Way to the Truth," *Education Week*, November 1, 2016, https://www.edweek.org/teaching-learning/opinion-why-students-cant-google-their-way-to-the-truth/2016/11.

10. Lori Robertson and Eugene Kiely, "How to Spot Fake News," FactCheck.org, November 18, 2016, http://www.factcheck.org/2016/11/how-to-spot-fake-news/.

11. Linda Elder, "Syllabus for Psychology 1," Foundation for Critical Thinking, December 2015, criticalthinking.org/pages/syllabus-psychology-i/459#top.

12. https://www.chronicle.com/article/scholars-talk-writing-sam-wineburg/

13. Donald Murray, "The Maker's Eye," in *Language Awareness: Readings for College Writers*, ed. Paul Eschholz, Alfred Rosa, and Virginia Clark, 8th ed. (Boston: Bedford/St. Martin's, 2000), 161–65.

4. Giving Feedback

1. See Christina Moore, "Frame Your Feedback: Making Peer Review Work in Class, Faculty Focus, June 6, 2016, facultyfocus.com/articles /teaching-and-learning/frame-feedback-making-peer-review-work-class/.

2. https://www.americanrhetoric.com/speeches/mlkihaveadream.htm

3. John Warner, *Why They Can't Write: Killing the Five-Paragraph Essay and Other Necessities* (Baltimore: Johns Hopkins University Press, 2018).

4. Richard Marius, *A Short Guide to Writing About History* (New York: HarperCollins, 1995), ix.

5. Helen Sword, *Stylish Academic Writing* (Cambridge, MA: Harvard University Press, 2012).

6. Andrew Cavanaugh and Liyan Song, "Audio Feedback Versus Written Feedback: Instructors' and Students' Perspectives," *MERLOT Journal of Online Learning and Teaching* 10, no. 1 (2014), 129, jolt.merlot.org/vol10no1 /cavanaugh_0314.pdf.

5. On (Not) Lecturing

1. Annie Murphy Paul, "Are College Lectures Unfair?" *New York Times*, September 12, 2015, https://www.nytimes.com/2015/09/13/opinion/sunday /are-college-lectures-unfair.html.

2. Ibid.

3. Peter N. Stearns, "Teaching and Learning in Lectures," in *History in Higher Education*, ed. Alan Booth and Paul Hyland (Oxford: Blackwell, 1996), 100.

4. "The Science of Learning in Action," University of Vermont website, Summer 2019, http://med.uvm.edu/vtmedicine/summer_2019/the_science _of_learning_in_action.

5. John Haas, "Students Today Don't Know Enough," History News Network, October 30, 2017, historynewsnetwork.org/article/167346.

6. I have never fully "flipped" a course, so I shall not pontificate on doing so here. For an explanation of how flipped classes work, see Stephanie Butler Velegol, Sarah E. Zappe, and Emily Mahoney, "Successful Flipped

Classes," *ASEE Prism* 24, no. 7 (2015), https://www.proquest.com/openview /f67db2dd3a363a6a55753bf4d26cbbb6/1?pq-origsite=gscholar&cbl=33050.

7. Karen Costa, "Four Ways to Keep Students' Attention," *Inside Higher Ed*, July 26, 2016, insidehighered.com/advice/2016/07/26/how-hold-students-att ention-classroom-essay, which references Carl Straumsheim, "Leave It in the Bag," *Inside Higher Ed*, May 13, 2016, https://www.insidehighered.com /news/2016/05/13/allowing-devices-classroom-hurts-academic-performance -study-finds.

8. Ben Yagoda, "Books and Mortar," *Chronicle of Higher Education*, November 30, 2015, chronicle.com/blogs/linguafranca/2015/11/30/books -and-mortar/.

9. Chris Berdik, "Dealing with Digital Distraction," The Hechinger Report, April 8, 2021, https://hechingerreport.org/dealing-digital-distraction/.

10. Adam Gazzaley and Larry D. Rosen, *The Distracted Mind: Ancient Brains in a High-Tech World* (Cambridge, MA: MIT Press, 2016), 137.

11. https://hechingerreport.org/dealing-digital-distraction/

6. Readings

1. Frank Furedi, "Focus Fracas," *Chronicle Review*, December 2015, chron icle.com/article/Focus-Fracas/234423.

2. Emma Pettit, "Does Reading on Computer Screens Affect Student Learning?" *Chronicle of Higher Education*, June 22, 2016, chronicle .com/article/Does-Reading-on-Computer/236879.

3. Note that this may preclude activities such as "flipping" your class or dividing students into groups or other activities as you will need to be more involved in helping students discover the connections between these seemingly disparate elements. To be sure, though, you can use class time to help students discover on their own the integration of your course via discussion, groups, and other non-lecture methods.

4. M.D.R. Evans et al., *Research in Social Stratification and Mobility*, Volume 28, Issue 2, June 2010, 171–97.

5. James M. Lang, *On Course* (Cambridge, MA: Harvard University Press, 2008), 51.

7. Why Test

1. Samuel Bowles and Herbert Gintis, *Schooling in Capitalist America* (New York: Basic Books, 1976).

2. Henry L. Roediger III and Jeffrey D. Karpicke, "The Power of Testing Memory: Basic Research and Implications for Educational Practice," *Perspectives on Psychological Science* 1, no.3 (2006): 181, 196. For a summary of this research, see Jessica Lahey, "Students Should Be Tested More, Not Less," *The Atlantic*, January 21, 2014, https://www.theatlantic.com/education /archive/2014/01/students-should-be-tested-more-not-less/283195/.

3. Roediger and Karpicke, "The Power of Testing Memory," 181, 196, 199.

8. How to Test

1. In some subjects, it might be appropriate to have a weekly quiz; in others, a test after each major unit. I suggest a minimum of three tests.

2. Before this next class, you should read and indeed take your own test. You may discover a misprint or ambiguity and can announce it yourself if no student catches it. You can also create an answer key for Part I, the short-answer section, and jot down your thoughts as to what points you expect to see made on the essay question(s). Doing so is crucial if you have TAs who will be doing any of the grading.

3. Assigning a numerical grade to students' second attempts can be tricky. What should Ernie receive if he got 76 the first time, then got everything right the second time? 88 is the average of 76 and 100, but is 88 fair, compared to students who got scores between 80 and 88 the first time? On the other hand, Ernie did outperform Suzie, who also got 76 on the first exam, then merely improved to 90 the second time, for an average of 83. I usually fiddle with the scores until I think I have everyone in a fair order. No one has ever complained; after all, they already had an extra chance to get a B.

4. You may of course discover that the question was bad and led to misinterpretation.

5. Often, I have little interest in grading or even reading third attempts, and I say so. If I have TAs, I might propose that the TA read the revision and certify to me that it answers the questions satisfactorily. Sometimes I suggest openly that the student seek out a fellow student who answered the items well, write down those answers, and make sure to understand why they are good answers. Such actions will yield a score of 70 for third attempts, much better than the D or F her first try garnered. A few students, in lieu

of making a third attempt on the exam, come up with creative alternative suggestions, which they then fulfill, earning better rewards than what they would've received otherwise.

6. Mastery learning is a strategy and educational philosophy first formally proposed by Benjamin Bloom in the late 1960s. The Wikipedia entry for "Mastery Learning" offers an adequate introduction to the topic, available at https://en.wikipedia.org/wiki/Mastery_learning.

7. Russell Means, "Fighting Words on the Future of the Earth," *Mother Jones*, December 1980, 25–31, 38.

8. Quoted in Linda B. Nilson, *Specifications Grading: Restoring Rigor, Motivating Students, and Saving Faculty Time* (Sterling, VA: Stylus, 2015), 26.

9. T.C. Toppino and H.A. Brochin, "Learning from Tests: The Case of True-False Examinations," *Journal of Educational Research* 83, no. 2 (1989): 119–24.

10. College Entrance Examination Board, *10 Real SATs* (New York: CEEB, 1995), 60.

11. ETS does not really take seriously its rationale for these items. This is evident from its "explanation" of this item, which tells students to focus on "key introductory and transitional words." Then "you will be able to eliminate several choices before you even think about the other blank." So much for understanding the logic of complex sentences! Ironically, the Princeton Review is much better than ETS at teaching students tricks like these. As a result, its coaching clinics result in significantly higher SAT scores. Since the Princeton Review is much more available to affluent suburbanites, it inadvertently helps justify the SAT by making its clients seem smarter.

12. High school grades offer the strongest single correlations with first-semester college grades.

13. Henry L. Roediger III and Jeffrey D. Karpicke, "The Power of Testing Memory: Basic Research and Implications for Educational Practice," *Perspectives on Psychological Science* 1, no. 3 (2006): 196.

14. Or, in this example of a U.S Census–based question, you might simply ask each student to find the number and calculate the percentage of white households in a certain county or zip code for a state in, say, 1970. This pushes each student to locate the appropriate census table and figure out how to calculate the percentage.

15. Often there is a logic to the order of your test items—perhaps the order in which your class took up that material. Be careful not to violate it.

16. Note from Nicholas Loewen: I was in my father's race relations class in 1992 and took his oral final. I still remember that the question I answered was about Chinese people in Mississippi and how they navigated that society.

9. Grading

1. Of course, there will be times when you can infer whose test it is, but those are fairly rare.

2. Or if the problem lies with ambiguity in the test item, write a better item next time.

3. Jeffrey Schinske and Kimberly Tanner, "Teaching More by Grading Less (or Differently)," *CBE—Life Sciences Education* 13, no. 2 (Summer 2014), ncbi.nlm.nih.gov/pmc/articles/PMC4041495/.

4. To review, the seven functions of testing are: (1) evaluation; (2) conveying the import of what's being taught; (3) motivating out-of-class coursework; (4) learning through test-taking; (5) giving feedback to students; (6) giving feedback to the instructor; and (7) motivating review of material taught thus far.

5. Ohmer Milton, Howard Pollio, and James Eison, *Making Sense of College Grades* (San Francisco: Jossey-Bass, 1986), quoted in Alfie Kohn, "The Dangerous Myth of Grade Inflation," *Chronicle of Higher Education* 49, no. 11 (2002): B7.

6. Quoted in Kohn, "The Dangerous Myth of Grade Inflation," B7.

7. Kohn, "The Dangerous Myth of Grade Inflation," B7.

8. Thomas M. Tripp et al., "The Fair Process Effect in the Classroom: Reducing the Influence of Grades on Student Evaluations of Teachers," *Journal of Marketing Education*, April 30, 2018, journals.sagepub.com/doi/abs/10.1177/0273475318772618.

9. www.insidehighered.com/news/2016/03/29/survey-finds-grade-inflation-continues-rise-four-year-colleges-not-community-college#

10. Teaching Diverse Students

1. Lester Lusher, "Teaching Assistants Like Me? Here's What Could Change," The Conversation, November 9, 2015, https://theconversation.com/teaching-assistants-like-me-heres-what-could-change-49269

2. Audrey Williams June, "Professors Are the Likeliest Mentors for Students, Except Those Who Aren't White," *Chronicle of Higher Educa-*

tion, October 30, 2018, chronicle.com/article/Professors-Are-the-Likeliest /244955.

3. See Project Implicit, www.implicit.harvard.edu.

4. Kathleen Tarr, "A Little More Every Day: How You Can Eliminate Bias in Your Own Classroom," *Chronicle of Higher Education*, September 23, 2015.

5. Thanks for this example and related ideas goes to James M. Lang, "A Welcoming Classroom," *Chronicle of Higher Education*, September 27, 2017, chronicle.com/article/A-Welcoming-Classroom/241294.

6. Katie Linder, "Student Uses and Perceptions of Closed Captions and Transcripts," Corvallis: Oregon State University Ecampus, 2016, https://go .3playmedia.com/rs-student.

7. Of course, all tests require time limit. I have often made two hours available for what I had intended as a one-hour test. No one has ever used more than about an hour and forty minutes.

8. Ken Bain, *What the Best College Teachers Do* (Cambridge, MA: Harvard Uiversity Press, 2004), 81–82.

9. Richard Arum and Josipa Roksa, *Academically Adrift: Limited Learning on College Campuses* (Chicago: University of Chicago Press, 2011), 130.

10. Jeremy Bauer-Wolf, "How to 'Not Be Rich,'" *Inside Higher Education*, April 16, 2018, insidehighered.com/news/2018/04/16/new-crowdsourced -student-affordability-guide-goes-viral-university-michigan, quoting and describing first-generation undergraduate Lauren Schandevel.

11. Ending Well

1. "The Lab" was the creation of my mentor, Dr. Ernst Borinski, a refugee from Hitler's Germany who taught at Tougaloo from 1947 until his death in 1983. Borinski was a remarkable man—an inspirational professor who used his status as an outsider to cross boundaries between white and Black Mississippi on behalf of social change. He is one of the main subjects of *From Swastika to Jim Crow*, a documentary and companion book that spawned a museum exhibit.

2. In promoting their disenfranchisement efforts in South Carolina, for example, Republicans cobbled together a collection of stories about individual fraudulent voters from other states to back their contention that their own state, in 2011, needed a new voter ID law. In reality, as historian Orville Vernon Burton noted in his expert witness report in the lawsuit challenging this

law, "no [South Carolina] bill sponsors, election administrators, or members of the testifying public could identify any verified instances of voter fraud that would be addressed by the voter ID law." "Direct Testimony of Dr. Orville Vernon Burton," *South Carolina v. United States*, U.S. Federal Court District of Columbia Case 1:12-cv-00203-CKK-BMK-JDB, https://law.osu.edu/ electionlaw/litigation/documents/WrittenDirectTestimonyofDrBurton.pdf.

About the Authors

James W. Loewen (1942–2021) was a bestselling and award-winning author. He won the American Book Award, the Oliver Cromwell Cox Award for Distinguished Anti-Racist Scholarship, the Spirit of America Award from the National Council for the Social Studies, and the Gustavus Myers Outstanding Book Award.

Nicholas Loewen teaches high school English in Washington, DC.

Michael Dawson is an independent sociologist who has taught at Portland Community College, Lewis & Clark College, Portland State University, and the University of Oregon. He is the author of *The Consumer Trap: Big Business Marketing in American Life.*

Publishing in the Public Interest

Thank you for reading this book published by The New Press; we hope you enjoyed it. New Press books and authors play a crucial role in sparking conversations about the key political and social issues of our day.

We hope that you will stay in touch with us. Here are a few ways to keep up to date with our books, events, and the issues we cover:

- Sign up at www.thenewpress.com/subscribe to receive updates on New Press authors and issues and to be notified about local events
- www.facebook.com/newpressbooks
- www.x.com/thenewpress
- www.instagram.com/thenewpress

Please consider buying New Press books not only for yourself, but also for friends and family and to donate to schools, libraries, community centers, prison libraries, and other organizations involved with the issues our authors write about.

The New Press is a 501(c)(3) nonprofit organization; if you wish to support our work with a tax-deductible gift please visit www.thenewpress.com/donate or use the QR code below.